Andrew Woods
Grace Romano

Oxford Grammar

Third Edition

Name:

Class:

4

OXFORD
UNIVERSITY PRESS

Contents

Topic 4: Sentences and punctuation

Topic 5: Using grammar

Topic 6: Extension and enrichment

Topic 1: Nouns, adjectives and noun groups

Learning intention

We are learning to use a variety of nouns, as well as expanding noun groups with adjectives, to add more precise, varied and engaging information about people, places and things.

Unit 1.1 Common nouns

Under the sea

Common nouns are ordinary nouns that name people, places, animals and things. *Fish, boat, sea, shark* and *sailor* are all common nouns.

1 On a separate piece of paper, write three common nouns from the picture opposite that:

a are smaller than you.
b are larger than you.
c are living things.
d are not living things.
e swim.
f float.

2 What am I?

a I have sharp teeth. I have a large, triangular fin on my back. ____________

b I am a machine. I sail underwater. ____________

c I am a water plant. Sometimes I wash up on the seashore. ____________

d I have eight tentacles. When scared, I squirt an inky liquid. ____________

e I am worn on the face to stop water getting in the eyes. ____________

3 Underline the words that you think are common nouns in each sentence. (The number of common nouns in each sentence is shown in brackets.)

a The shark swam in and out of the shipwreck. (2)

b Beautiful fish hurried past the colourful coral. (2)

c An octopus ignored the submarine as it glided slowly towards the seabed. (3)

d The divers reached the ledge with plenty of air left in their tanks. (4)

e High above, a lone dolphin leapt over the buoy. (2)

Only use a capital letter to begin a **common noun** if that word begins a sentence.

4 Unjumble these common nouns from the picture.

a ngyoxe knats ____________

b kpiwsechr ____________

c bsurmaine ____________

d gihsfni abot ____________

Try it out!

On a separate piece of paper, write a list of 50 **common nouns** that you can see from your chair.

The Melons' photo album

Honey Dew

Melaneeza

Paddy

Gourdy

Melon Patch

Minnie Lee

Rocky and Walter

Rufus, the Melon Collie

Cantaloupe Lane

Chunky Mellow Chocs

Muskmelon Maulers

River Vine Queen and Cucurbit River

Proper nouns are special names for people, places and things. Proper nouns always begin with a capital letter. For example: *Samir Katie Cantaloupe Lane Friday Melbourne October*

1 You can see some photos from the Melon family's photo album opposite. The photos tell us about the lives of the Melons.

For example: *The Melons barrack for the Muskmelon Maulers rugby team.*

Use the photos to help you to make up three statements about the Melons. Remember that proper nouns must begin with a capital letter.

____

____

____

2 Rewrite this sentence, correcting the proper nouns.

Grandma minnie lee melon took her grandchildren, rocky, walter and honey dew, on a fishing trip along the cucurbit river in her boat, *river vine queen.*

____

____

____

3 Complete this table of proper nouns, using names that begin with the letter that appears at the start of each row.

	Boy's name	Girl's name	Place (town, country, etc.)
M	Mark		
E			Eaglehawk
L			
O		Olga	
N			
S			

4 Circle the words that should begin with a capital letter.

a My sister anna likes to hear mother goose nursery rhymes before she goes to sleep.

b "Hey dad!" i called out to my father. "where are you going?"

c The home of the prime minister, called the lodge, is not far from parliament house.

Try it out!

On a separate piece of paper, write **proper noun** place names starting with each letter of your full name. For example: *Mick Smith = Melbourne Inglewood Canberra Kuwait Sydney Maroochydore Ireland Tenterfield Hungary*

(Note: If there is an X in your name, the X can be anywhere in the place name.)

Having an idea!

1 ______________________

2 ______________________

3 ______________________

4 ______________________

5 ______________________

6 ______________________

7 ______________________

8 ______________________

9 ______________________

Concrete nouns are the names of things we can see and touch.
For example: *chair, apple, tree, building*
Abstract nouns are the names of ideas and feelings. These things cannot be seen or touched.
For example: *honesty, love, freedom, music*

1 The nouns in the box are abstract nouns. Write them beneath the photos on the opposite page that they best match.

love speed childhood sleep friendship
anger joy sadness envy

2 Draw circles around the abstract nouns in these proverbs.

The numbers in brackets tell how many **abstract nouns** are in the proverb.

- **a** Honesty is the best policy. (2)
- **b** Curiosity killed the cat. (1)
- **c** Charity begins at home. (1)
- **d** Strength grows stronger by being tried. (1)
- **e** Loyalty is worth more than money. (1)
- **f** Beauty is only skin deep. (1)

3 Change these adjectives or verbs to abstract nouns. For example: *sleepy – sleep*

a brave ____________ **b** laugh ____________

c know ____________ **d** able ____________

e delightful ____________ **f** silly ____________

4 Draw lines to match abstract nouns that are antonyms (opposites).

bravery wealth honesty failure strength

success deceit poverty weakness cowardice

Try it out!

Write a sentence containing one of these **abstract nouns**.
opinion, happiness, courage, talent, luck

____

____

A Viking tale of wives, loaves and elves

Read this story.

Once upon a time – for that is how tales start – there were three Viking wives who baked six loaves. They carefully wrapped the loaves in beautiful silken scarves and placed them carefully upon the shelves of the kitchen.

Passing by were five elves riding magnificent wolves. The elves stole the loaves that the wives had just finished baking.

The wives, with sharpened kitchen knives in hand, climbed onto their spotted calves and chased those thieves.

The elves rode for their lives.

The elves found that they could not outrun the wives so they split the loaves into halves. They hid half under some leaves and the rest they left for the wives to find.

The wives, who were running late for their Viking Association meeting, said, "Oh well, half a loaf is better than no bread." And on they went with their Viking lives.

To make plural nouns of most words ending in *f* or *fe*, change the *f* or *fe* to *v* and then add *es*.
For example: *elf – elves* *calf – calves* *life – lives*

1 Circle the words in the story that have changed from *f* or *fe* to *v* to become plural nouns.

2 Change these nouns to plural nouns.

a loaf ________ **b** half ________ **c** wolf ________
d life ________ **e** wife ________ **f** scarf ________
g knife ________ **h** leaf ________ **i** thief ________
j shelf ________ **k** self ________ **l** yourself ________

For some words ending in *f*, just add *s* to form plural nouns.
For example: *roof – roofs*

3 Just add *s* to change these nouns to plural nouns.

a chef ________ **b** chief ________ **c** reef ________
d cliff ________ **e** belief ________ **f** puff ________

Do you remember these plural noun rules? You will need to know them to complete the exercises on this page.
For some words just add **s**.
For words ending in **ch**, **sh**, **ss**, **s** or **x** add **es**.
For words ending in **y** following a consonant, change the **y** to **i** and then add **es**.
For words ending in **ay**, **ey** or **oy** just add **s**.

4 Change the following nouns to plural nouns.

a tiger ________ **b** marsh ________ **c** army ________
d gas ________ **e** cherry ________ **f** knife ________
g valley ________ **h** student ________ **i** leaf ________

5 On a separate piece of paper, change each of the following groups of words to plural nouns and then write sentences containing each group.
For example: *leaf, cherry, box*
After we had packed the cherries into boxes, we raked up leaves.

a monkey, loaf, dish, box **b** city, chimney, life

Try it out!

On a separate piece of paper, write a short story in which you include the **plural nouns** of *witch, shelf, thief, key, peach, alley, fairy, journey* and *jelly*.

Adjectives

Harry the Monster

IDENTIKIT description:

____________ head	____________ ears	____________ fangs
____________ nose	____________ body	____________ skin
____________ left arm	____________ forearms	____________ waist
____________ brow	____________ legs	____________ trousers
____________ claws		

Adjectives tell us more about nouns. They describe people, places, animals, things and ideas.
For example: *The tired old man sat with his faithful dog.*
Which words describe the man? (*tired, old*) Which word describes the dog? (*faithful*)
In this sentence, *tired, old* and *faithful* are the adjectives.

1 The monster hunters need to complete their IDENTIKIT picture of Harry the Monster. Use the adjectives in the box to complete a description of the wanted monster on the IDENTIKIT form.

floppy sharp spotty furrowed hairy
bald thick hooked bandy tattooed
muscular huge cuffed cargo

Some words that are usually nouns may also be used as adjectives.
For example: **a flower garden, bed covers**
Some adjectives are formed from nouns.
For example:
anger – angry,
taste – tasty,
fun – funny

2 Circle the adjectives that mean the same as the bold words.

a **huge** gigantic tiny large mammoth enormous

b **thin** broad skinny lanky plump slender

c **hooked** true crooked curved straight bent

d **muscular** feeble strong brawny weak powerful

3 Tick the adjectives that you think best describe Harry the Monster.

☐ gentle	☐ ferocious	☐ affectionate	☐ peaceful	☐ kind
☐ fierce	☐ cheerful	☐ violent	☐ angry	☐ jolly
☐ meek	☐ harmless	☐ helpful	☐ dangerous	☐ wild
☐ vicious	☐ savage	☐ friendly	☐ ruthless	☐ mean

4 Use adjectives to rewrite these sentences in an improved way.

a The monster destroyed the village. ______________________

____

b On the table was a feast of sandwiches, fruit, ice cream and lemonade.

____

____

Try it out!

On a separate piece of paper, write as many **adjectives** as you can think of to describe one of the following: *a winter's day, a summer's day, a dog, a cat, a ride on a roller coaster.*

Five hairy monsters

Five hairy monsters sat down to lunch,
Buttered bits of concrete, munch, munch, munch.
One swats a busy bee sitting on its paw,
Falls off his creaky chair, leaving four.

Four savage monsters sat down for tea,
Jam on a joke book with roast fiddle-dee.
One starts a-giggling, tee-hee-hee,
Laughs himself silly and that leaves three.

Three mean monsters ready for supper,
Sawdust and glue and an icy-cold cuppa.
One takes a huge bite and tries to chew,
But his jaws get stuck and that leaves two.

Two hungry monsters wake for a feed,
Nothing in the pantry so it's agreed –
That those two monsters, each a brother,
Munch on a brekky of one another.

OXFORD UNIVERSITY PRESS

Adjectives are words that describe nouns. Adjectives tell us more about people, places, animals, things and ideas. We often expand noun groups by adding adjectives.

1 Which adjectives in the poem "Five hairy monsters" tell us about these nouns?

a bits of concrete ____________ b chair ____________

c monsters ____________

d bee ____________ e cuppa ____________

f bite ____________ g book ____________

h jaws ____________

2 Write number adjectives for these nouns. For example: *two arms*

a ____________ monsters b ____________ paws

c ____________ chair legs d ____________ days (in a week)

3 Match the adjectives describing nationality with the nouns in the box.

dragon bagpipes kimono boomerang elephant pyramids

a Scottish ____________ b Australian ____________

c Chinese ____________ d Japanese ____________

e Egyptian ____________ f African ____________

4 Underline the noun groups and colour the adjectives in these sentences.

a The fierce bushfire was brought under control by the brave, hard-working firefighters.

b Tammy was a naughty dog for chasing the frightened sheep.

c Deep in the wild woods, the slumbering dragon stirred from his long sleep at the sound of the huge explosion.

5 Change these nouns to adjectives that can be found in the poem.

a hair ____________ b butter ____________

c hunger ____________ d ice ____________

Try it out!

On a separate piece of paper, rewrite these sentences using **adjectives** to expand the **noun groups**, making them more interesting.

On the street, the trams and cars are like insects before a storm.

The tiger stalked the goat through the jungle.

Welcome to Country

Have you ever been to an important event, such as a special celebration or a sporting grand final? If you have, then before the event started you may have seen and heard a **Welcome to Country**.

A **Welcome to Country** might involve dancing, music or a smoking ceremony (in which native plants are burned to produce smoke that wards off bad spirits from the people and the land).

The most important part of a **Welcome to Country** is spoken by an Elder from a First Nations community.

There are many First Nations communities across Australia. Each community has boundaries around their traditional lands. The boundaries are not fences or walls or lines marked on a map. They are the mountain ranges and waterways – the natural features of the land. When someone wants to cross into the traditional land of a First Nations community, they are given permission in the form of a **Welcome to Country**.

The traditional land of the Wurundjeri people is Melbourne and its surrounds. Aunty Joy Murphy Wandin is the Senior Elder of the Wurundjeri people. She has given the **Welcome to Country** on many occasions for more than 40 years, and has helped to raise awareness and understanding of reconciliation with First Nations people.

1. Circle the noun groups in these sentences from the "Welcome to Country" text.
   - a. Have you ever been to an important event like a special celebration or a sporting grand final?
   - b. There are many First Nations communities across Australia.
   - c. The traditional land of the Wurundjeri people is Melbourne and its surrounds.

Remember, a noun group usually contains an adjective and a noun.

2. Write four proper nouns that have been used in the "Welcome to Country" text.

_______________ _______________

_______________ _______________

3. Write adjectives from the "Welcome to Country" text to complete these noun groups.

   - a. _______________ ranges
   - b. _______________ features
   - c. _______________ celebration
   - d. _______________ lands
   - e. _______________ plants
   - f. _______________ spirits

4. Change the following common nouns to plural nouns.
   - a. boundary _______________
   - b. community _______________
   - c. ceremony _______________
   - d. country _______________

Try it out!

Write an **abstract noun** from the box that might name a feeling or idea to match the following sentences.

delight bravery pride

- a. What Aunty Joy Murphy Wandin is feeling as she performs a Welcome to Country _______________
- b. How you might feel if your team is playing in a grand final _______________
- c. What a surf lifesaver might show as she enters the ocean to rescue a struggling swimmer _______________

Topic 1: Test your grammar

Nouns, adjectives and noun groups

1 Shade the bubble next to the **common noun**.

○ gigantic ○ villain ○ swam ○ silently

2 Shade the bubble next to the correct **plural noun** for **knife**.

○ knifes ○ knifies ○ knivies ○ knives

3 Shade the bubble next to the **proper noun**.

○ manager ○ Wilson Street ○ mountain ○ giraffe

4 Shade the bubble next to the **concrete noun**.

○ kindness ○ despair ○ factory ○ humour

5 Shade the bubble next to the **abstract noun**.

○ cry ○ sorrow ○ unhappy ○ sad

6 Shade the bubble below the **abstract noun** in this sentence.

The children's enthusiasm for the project astonished Mrs Barindji.

○ ○ ○ ○

7 Shade the bubble next to the correct **plural noun** for **fairy**.

○ fairys ○ fairies ○ faires ○ faireys

8 Shade the bubble next to the **type of noun** represented by these naming words.

talent, mercy, skill, intelligence

◯ common ◯ proper ◯ abstract ◯ concrete

9 Shade the bubble below the **adjective** in this sentence.

We had to hold on to our hats in the gusty wind.

◯ ◯ ◯ ◯

10 Shade the bubble next to the word that can be used as a noun or an **adjective**.

◯ safe ◯ chilly ◯ safely ◯ narrow

11 Shade the bubble next to the **adjective**.

◯ think ◯ wild ◯ blew ◯ write

12 Shade the bubble next to the noun group that contains an **adjective**.

◯ an enchanting story ◯ a diamond ◯ an elephant ◯ the sunset

How am I doing?

Tick the boxes if you understand.

- Common nouns are ordinary nouns that name people, places, animals and things. ☐
- Proper nouns are special nouns for people, places and things. ☐
- Concrete nouns name things we can touch and see. ☐
- Abstract nouns are names for ideas and feelings. ☐
- Many nouns must change to form plural nouns. ☐
- Adjectives describe nouns. They can be used with nouns to form noun groups. ☐

Topic 2: Verbs, adverbs, prepositions and phrases

Learning intention

We are learning to identify and use verbs, adverbs, prepositions and phrases to make our writing more interesting and detailed.

Unit 2.1 Doing verbs

Verberella

Poor Cindy spends her days mopping, scrubbing, wiping, dusting, washing, vacuuming, polishing and daydreaming.

She dreams that one day she will become The Girl of Steel Wool – Verberella!

Verberella leaps over tall buildings.

She blows fire from her mouth.

She flies like a jet-fighter.

She lifts boulders with one hand and then smashes them with the other hand.

She tosses bad guys aside.

Then Cindy realises that she doesn't need to change who she is and doesn't need superpowers. With her brain and imagination, she can do anything.

Doing verbs tell us what is being done in a sentence. They tell us about the action.
For example: *The whale swam. I heard them arrive.*
What did the whale do? *It swam.* What did I do? *I heard. Swam* and *heard* are doing verbs.

1 Read "Verberella" and find doing verbs that could fill the gaps in these sentences.

a Verberella ______________________ over tall buildings.

b Verberella ______________________ boulders with one hand.

c With her other hand Verberella ______________________ boulders.

d Verberella ______________________ like a jet-fighter.

e She ______________________ bad guys aside.

f She ______________________ fire from her mouth.

2 Rewrite these words as doing verbs by adding the ending *ing*.

a (Just add *ing*.) lift ______________________, wash ______________________,
toss ________________, leap ________________, daydream ________________

b (Double the last letter.) mop ________________, cut ________________,
clap ________________, scrub ________________, rub ________________

c (Drop the final *e*.) wipe ________________, bite ________________,
ride ________________, race ________________,
wriggle ________________

3 Write six doing verbs that tell us what Cindy does and six doing verbs that tell us what Verberella does.

Cindy ____

____

Verberella ____

____

Some words can be verbs or nouns. For example: **I am washing. I hung out the washing. I wish I was famous. I made a wish.**

Try it out!

On a separate piece of paper, write 20 **doing verbs** that tell us something about the way different parts of your body act.
For example: *my toes wriggle, my eyes stare, I clench my fist*

Danny Verb

Danny buckles on his kneepads.

He slides into his boots.

He checks and then puts on his elbow pads.

Finally, Danny slips in his mouthguard.

Verbs tell us what is happening or being done in the sentence.
For example: *Danny* ***skates*** *down the road.*
What does Danny do? *Danny skates.* (*Skates* is the verb.)

1 Read "Danny Verb" and then underline the doing verbs below that tell us what is being done.

a Danny buckles on his kneepads.
b Danny slides into his boots.
c He checks his elbow pads.
d Danny slips in his mouthguard.
e Danny takes a tumble.
f He pulls on his helmet.

Sometimes verbs can be more than one word. We call these verb groups.
For example: *was running, is skating, are sliding, will tumble*

2 Look around your classroom and write down three sentences containing two-word verbs that tell what people are doing. Underline the verb groups in your sentences.

For example: *Jason* ***is sitting*** *at his table. Nick and Carmel* ***are talking****.*

3 Match the occupations with their most likely verbs. For example: *A pilot flies.*

Occupations	Verbs
mechanic	serves
author	operates
waiter	repairs
surgeon	sells
salesperson	plays
musician	writes

When *having* or *being* words are used on their own, we call them relating verbs.
Having words: *had, have, has.* Being words: *am, are, is, was, were, will, shall, be.*
For example: *The skateboard* ***is*** *on the shelf. Danny* ***has*** *kneepads. I* ***am*** *here. We* ***are*** *happy.*

4 Write the sentence from the comic strip that contains a relating verb.

5 Choose a relating verb from the box above and write it in a sentence of your own.

Try it out!

Create a verb poster by collecting images of actions and then labelling the pictures with verbs.

Limericks

A scientist named Ted Maclean
Invented a time machine
Took a trip to the past
Said, "I'm sure this won't last."
Then vanished and has not been seen.

Matilda from Woolloomooloo
Liked to bathe in a product called Gloo
But she ran out of luck
One day and got stuck
On the fur-lined seat of her loo.

Now Badir from Bendigo
Instead scrubbed himself with Velcro
He'd rubbity-dub
And scrubbity-scrub
'Til his mum cried, "Where'd that boy go?"

An Australian player of old
His name being Fred I am told
Once let go a flipper
A rippety-dipper
And found himself out! Cleanly bowled!

Saying verbs are verbs that show the manner in which something is being spoken or has been spoken. For example: *giggled, replied, groaning, says, said*

1 Read "Limericks" and look for clues to help you circle the saying verbs in these sentences.

a "I'm sure this won't last," said Tarun.

b "Help, I'm stuck!" screamed Matilda.

c "Where'd that boy go?" cried Badir's mum.

d I was told the player's name was Fred. (Be careful!)

Remember, a verb can be made up of more than one word.

2 Write suitable saying verbs from the box in the sentences below.

asked sighed shouted groaned suggested laughed

a "I'm bored!" ______________________ Rupert.

b "Where'd you buy your new backpack?" ______________________ Samira.

c Mr Cruz ______________________ for the boys to paddle back to the beach.

d "Not maths again!" ______________________ the children.

e The audience ______________________ hysterically at the comedian's punchline.

f "Why don't you turn it around this way?" ______________________ the science teacher.

3 Select three of the following saying verbs and, on a separate piece of paper, write sentences of your own.

giggled complained growled replied whispered cried yelled

Try it out!

Read this well-known limerick and then circle the **saying verb** in it.

An epicure dining at Crewe
Found a rather large mouse in his stew.
Cried the waiter, "Don't shout
And wave it about,
Or the rest will be wanting one too!"

(An epicure is a person with refined taste in food and drink.)

New school

from *Smile* by Raina Telgemeier

Thinking and feeling verbs show what we think, believe or feel about things. They commonly express an opinion on something.

For example: *"I know what I'll do next,"* ***thought*** *Briana.*

We ***like*** *to ride our bikes after school.*

1 Read the comic strip, then use the thinking and feeling verbs from the box to complete the sentences.

remembered   wondered   enjoyed   thought

a Raina ______________________ her new school was the same as the old one.

b The other students ______________________ their summer.

c Raina's mother ______________________ how Raina's day had gone.

d They laughed when they ______________________ *Nightmare on Elm Street*.

2 Draw circles around the thinking or feeling verbs in these sentences.

a Do you believe in flying saucers?

b The scientist concluded that climate change was a reality.

c "I think I'll have the orange one," decided Ahmed.

d "My son likes tennis," said Mrs Morales.

Thinking and feeling verbs are sometimes called sensing verbs.

3 Use three of the thinking and feeling verbs below to write sentences of your own.

love, hate, felt, trust, enjoy

____

____

____

Try it out!

Write three things you might wish for if you had a magic lamp.

In each of your sentences, use the **thinking** and **feeling verb wish**.

____

____

____

Willa's time bubble travel map

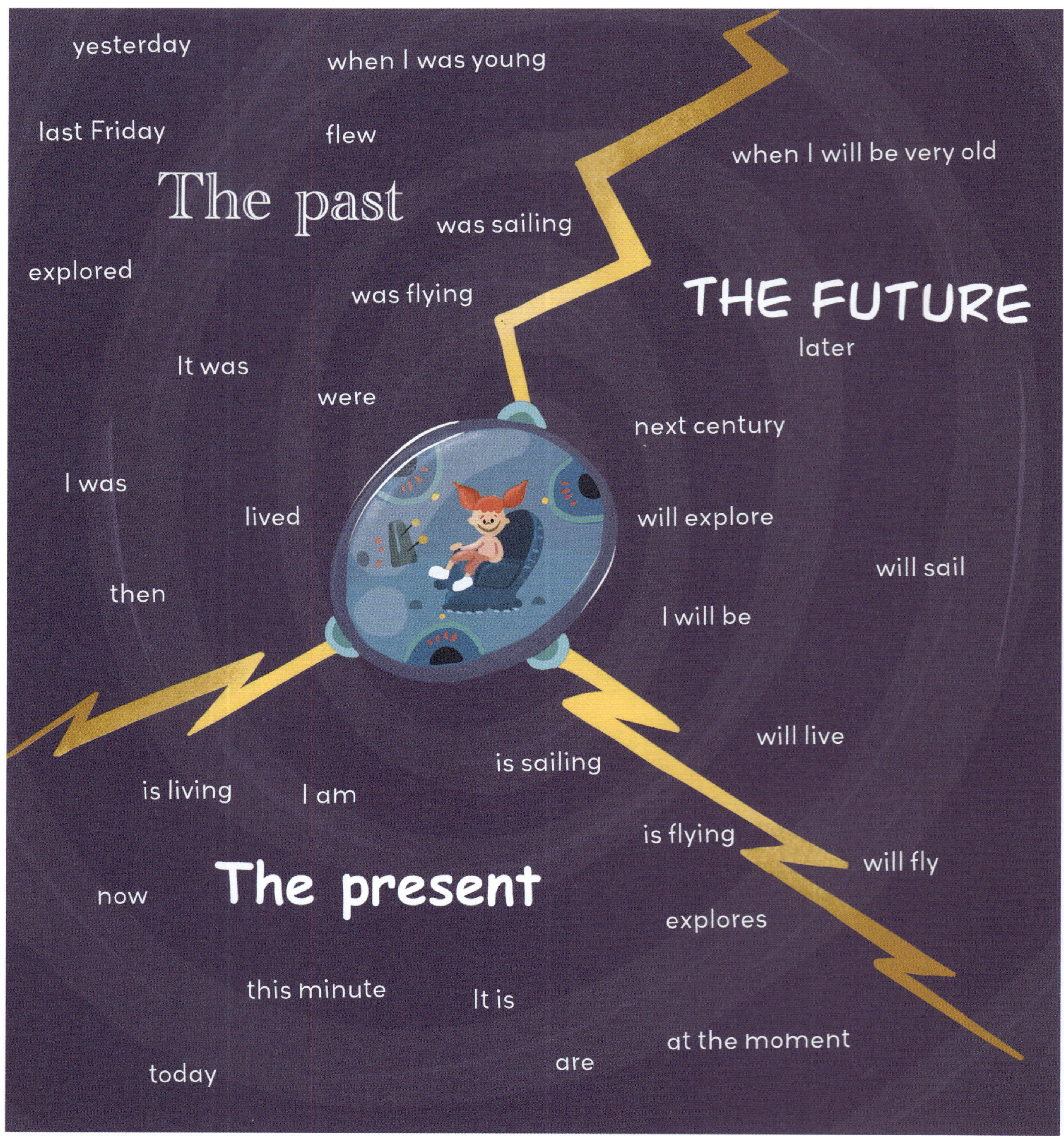

Verbs can show us whether something has happened (past), is happening (present) or will happen (future). We call this the verb tense.

1 Read "Willa's time bubble travel map" and then add the correct verb tense to complete the table.

Past	**Present**	**Future**
I was	I am	I ______
______	______	will live
______	is sailing	______
flew	______	______
______	explores	______

The word tense comes from the Latin word *tempus*, meaning "time". When we talk about the tense of a verb, we are talking about the time that the action in the sentence has taken place.

2 Write whether these extracts from Willa's diary are about the past, present or future.

a I am adjusting the radar. It needs a twist and a wrench. ______

b We will arrive in ten minutes. I will send my robot cats X-Port and M-Port out of the bubble first. ______

c I travelled back to when dinosaurs roamed Australia. I saw a muttaburrasaurus eating plants. ______

3 Change these sentences to the past tense.

a I am drinking my milkshake. ______

b The cat will creep slowly towards the unsuspecting bird. ______

______

4 Change these sentences to the present tense.

a I will throw the basketball to you. ______

b The dancers came onto the stage. ______

______

Try it out!

Imagine some of the things Willa might see and do on her time-travelling journeys. Using "Willa's time bubble travel map", write three sentences in her diary (use a separate piece of paper). Write one sentence about the **past**, one about the **present** and one about the **future**. What things would you do if you could travel in a time bubble?

Scorch

YOU might be feeling TIRED AND LISTLESS!

YOU could be low on energy levels!

YOU may need a pick-me-up!

Perhaps YOU would benefit from a ***NEW***, exciting, healthy drink

... if so, then ...

... YOU should drink ***SCORCH***

SCORCH – it will certainly perk up YOUR day!

Scorch is definitely made from all-natural ingredients: 100% water! Go plastic-free and drink it from the tap!

Some verbs help us to express ideas about what is possible. These verbs are called modal verbs.
For example: *might, may, can, will, ought to, could, should, would, need to*

1 Read the advertisement for "Scorch" to help you complete these sentences with modal verbs.

Modal verbs are never used alone. They are helping (auxiliary) verbs.

a You ______________________ benefit from a new drink.

b You ______________________ be feeling tired.

c Scorch ______________________ certainly perk up your day.

d People who are low on energy levels ______________________ enjoy Scorch.

e For an exciting and healthy drink you ______________________ drink Scorch.

Modal adverbs are words that tell us to what degree something will or won't happen.
For example: *I probably won't watch television tonight. It's possibly going to rain tomorrow.*

2 There are three modal adverbs in the advertisement. Write them on the line below.

____

3 Draw circles around the modal verbs in these sentences.

a I might go to the movies tonight.

b "You should take an umbrella with you," suggested Seth.

c "You must have a good memory," said Mrs Wang.

4 Select a modal adverb from the box and write it in a sentence.

obviously	apparently	arguably	possibly	hardly	definitely

____

____

____

Try it out!

Persuasive texts such as the advertisement for "Scorch" often use the pronouns *you, we* or *us* to include and appeal to the audience. With a partner, write a short advertisement on a separate piece of paper. Include the pronouns *you, we* or *us* and some **modal verbs** and **adverbs**.

The adventures of Adverb Man

This looks like another job for ADVERB MAN!

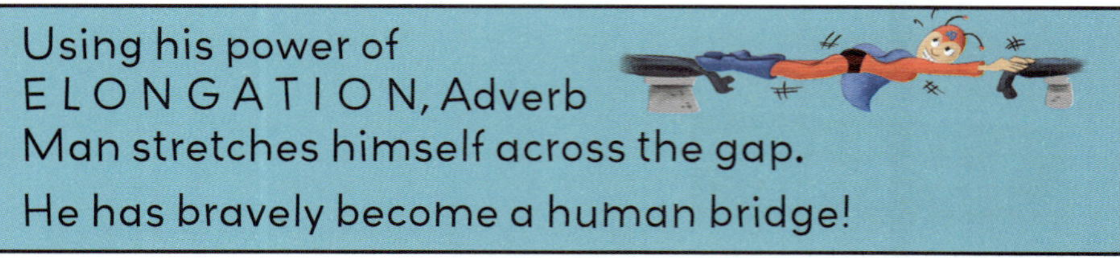

Adverbs add details about verbs. For example: *She writes* ***neatly***.

Many adverbs end in *ly* (*quickly, carefully*) but some don't (*later, here, fast*).
Adverbs often tell *how, when* or *where*.

For example: *The boat glided* ***slowly***. (How did the boat glide? *slowly*)

The train is arriving ***later***. (When is the train arriving? *later*)

The rabbit stopped ***here***. (Where did the rabbit stop? *here*)

Adverbs can also add details to adjectives or other adverbs. For example: **She is a really neat writer.** OR **She writes really neatly.**

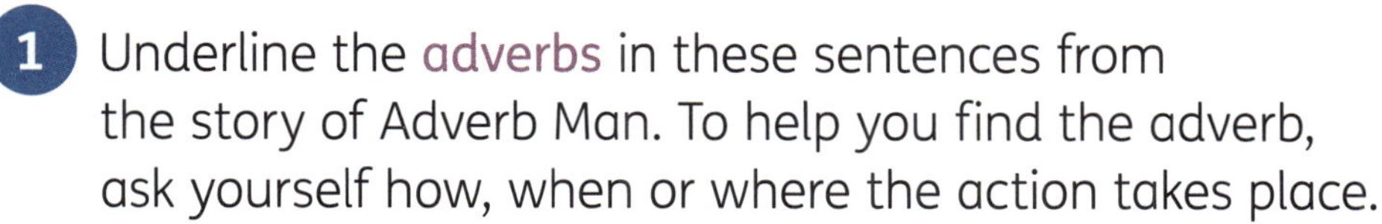

1 Underline the adverbs in these sentences from the story of Adverb Man. To help you find the adverb, ask yourself how, when or where the action takes place.

- **a** The train slowly leaves the station.
- **b** Soon it is rumbling quickly through the countryside.
- **c** The bridge has collapsed suddenly.
- **d** The train speeds onwards.
- **e** The passengers chat happily.
- **f** The train rapidly approaches the bridge.
- **g** The passengers are completely unaware of the fate that awaits them.
- **h** Adverb Man has bravely become a human bridge.

2 Use adverbs from the story that tell us more about Adverb Man.

- **a** How does Adverb Man assess the situation? ______________________
- **b** How does Adverb Man fly to the scene? ______________________
- **c** How does Adverb Man become a human bridge? ______________________
- **d** How does Adverb Man complete another job? ______________________

3 Write an adverb from the box that can be used to replace the **bold** words below.
For example: *We crossed the road* **with great care**. (carefully)

peacefully	softly	easily	here	quietly	soon

- **a** The thieves approached the doorway **in a quiet way**. ______________________
- **b** She answered the question **in a soft voice**. ______________________
- **c** Mark and Irene will arrive **in a short while**. ______________________
- **d** The baby slept **in peace** during the violent hailstorm. ______________________
- **e** The watch was found **in this place**. ______________________
- **f** Harvey won the race **with ease**. ______________________

Try it out!

On a separate piece of paper, write **adverbs** that tell how you do these things:
run, work, sleep, walk, swim, climb, play

Preppo Boy returns

From his lookout above his hideout Preppo Boy spots trouble.

A billy-cart is speeding down a steep slope and seems to be headed straight for a tree.

Quick as a flash, Preppo Boy is on the scene. With nerves of steel he stands in the path of the hurtling cart.

He stops the billy-cart just before the tree. Another billy-cart rushes past the tree.

In billy-cart number 7 is a very angry Nicky Woops.

In billy-cart number 5 is the winner of this year's Fantastic Billy-Cart Downhill Derby – a very happy Dom Blamey.

In the sky and flying faster than a speeding bullet to his hideout is Preppo Boy – with a very red face.

Prepositions are small connecting words. Prepositions connect nouns, pronouns or phrases to other words within a sentence.

For example: *The girl is **on** the swing.*

The word *on* tells us where, and it connects the girl and the swing.

1 Here is a list of the most common prepositions. Circle the 11 prepositions from the list that are also in the story about Preppo Boy.

about	above	across	after	against	along	around
at	before	below	beneath	beside	between	by
down	for	from	in	into	near	of
off	on	over	past	through	to	towards
under	until	up	upon	with		

2 Use prepositions to complete these phrases from the story.

a ________ billy-cart number 5

b ____________ nerves of steel

c ____________________ a tree

d ________________ his lookout

e _______________ his hideout

f __________________ the path

g __________________ the tree

h _________________ the scene

i ______________ a steep slope

j ____________________ the sky

k _______________ his hideout

l ____________ a very red face

Sometimes two **prepositions** are used together. For example: **away from, down into, along with**

3 Underline the prepositions in each sentence.

a The cat climbed over the fence.

b We were asked to wait until the bell rang.

c The billy-cart hurtled towards the tree.

d She left her umbrella near the doorway.

e The boats passed between the flags and headed into the bay.

f The fox's den was hidden under the bridge.

Try it out!

On a separate piece of paper, rewrite the sentences below as many times as you can, giving them a different meaning by changing only the **prepositions**.

For example: *The jar was **on** the table. The jar was **under** the table.*

The billy-cart crashed beside a tree.

She jumped into the creek.

We ate pizza during the show.

The robber ran along the road.

The Moon

The Moon has a face like the clock in the hall;
She shines on thieves on the garden wall,
On streets and fields and harbour quays,
And birdies asleep in the forks of the trees.

The squalling cat and the squeaking mouse,
The howling dog by the door of the house,
The bat that lies in bed at noon,
All love to be out by the light of the Moon.

But all of the things that belong to the day
Cuddle to sleep to be out of her way;
And flowers and children close their eyes
Till up in the morning the sun shall arise.

Robert Louis Stevenson

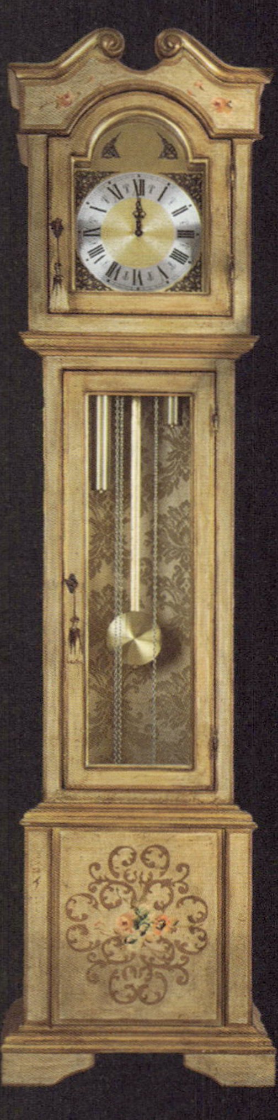

Phrases are groups of words without verbs. Phrases help to make sentences more interesting. Phrases tell us when, where and how. Phrases that begin with a preposition are called prepositional phrases.

For example: *The wind howled. The wind howled* ***during the night***. (when)

The wind howled ***through the open window***. (where) *The wind howled* ***with frightening force***. (how)

1 Use the poem "The Moon" to help you underline the prepositional phrase in each of these sentences and write whether it tells **when**, **where** or **how**.

a The clock was in the hall. ______________________

b The bat sleeps at noon. ______________________

c The birdies sleep in the forks of trees. ______________________

Phrases can come at the end, at the beginning or in the middle of sentences.

2 Complete the sentences below using prepositional phrases from the box.

in an angry voice	in the morning	on the classroom display board

a We pinned our projects ______________________.

b The bus will be departing ______________________.

c The giant demanded more food ______________________.

3 Complete the sentences below using prepositional phrases from the box.

Beside the swaggie	Near the council offices	Without hesitation

a ______________________ the lifesaver plunged into the raging surf.

b ______________________ protestors waved their signs.

c ______________________ walked his faithful dog, Blue.

4 Underline the prepositional phrases in these sentences.

a My alarm clock always rings at six o'clock.

b We saw a very funny clown at the circus.

c Three possums sat on the leafy branch munching the fruit.

Try it out!

On a separate piece of paper, write your own **phrases** to complete the sentences.

a We followed **b** The horse cantered **c** The storm struck

Somali food

Is ka warran!

In the Somali language that means "Hello" and "How are you?"

My name is Najaha. My family came to live in Australia five years ago. Let me share some of my favourite Somali meals with you.

For breakfast, my family eats *anjero* or *muufo.* They are homemade pancakes. Sometimes we might fry some *bur*, which are doughnuts made from flour, coconut milk powder, yeast, sugar and cardamom.

Lunch is the main meal of the day for my family.

We are a Muslim family so we only eat *halal* meals (*halal* means that the food can be eaten according to our Islamic religion). We do not eat pork products such as ham or bacon. Our lunch may be goat meat, chicken or fish with rice or even pasta.

For a snack, we occasionally eat *sambusas*, which are pastries filled with meat, onion, herbs and spices.

On special feast days, such as Eid al-Fitr, which we celebrate at the end of our fasting month of Ramadan, we eat treats. My favourite is when we make *halwa. Halwa* is a very sweet treat. It tastes delicious, so whenever it is served we gobble it up greedily.

Remember: Some verbs can be **doing** or **saying verbs**. Adverbs add details about verbs. When a preposition is followed by a noun or noun group we call it a prepositional phrase.

1 Underline the doing verbs in these sentences from the "Somali food" text.

a My family came to live in Australia five years ago.

b For breakfast my family eats *anjero* or *muufo*.

c Whenever *halwa* is served we gobble it up greedily.

2 Circle the saying verbs in these sentences.

a "My name is Najaha," said the young girl.

b "Do you fast for the whole month of Ramadan?" asked the journalist.

c "It tastes delicious!" exclaimed Najaha.

3 Use the "Somali food" text to help you write adverbs to complete the following sentences.

a We ______________________________ eat *halal* meals.

b It tastes delicious, so ______________ it is served we gobble it up ______________ .

c For a snack, we ______________________________ eat *sambusas*.

4 Underline the prepositional phrases in these sentences.

a A huge dish of *halwa* was placed upon the table.

b In the distance we could see the parade of circus entertainers marching around the bend.

c People of many different cultures have settled throughout Australia.

d *Sambusas* are pastries filled with meat, onion, herbs and spices.

Try it out!

On a separate piece of paper, write sentences about food containing these **thinking** and **feeling verbs**.

wonder *imagine* *enjoy* *dislike*

Topic 2: Test your grammar

Verbs, adverbs and prepositional phrases

1 Shade the bubble next to the **doing verb**.

○ crept ○ hero ○ quietly ○ spider

2 Shade the bubble below the **doing verb** in this sentence.

A thief stole the precious diamonds from the museum.

○ ○ ○ ○

3 Shade the bubble below the **relating verb** in this sentence.

The suitcase with the red ribbon was on the carousel.

○ ○ ○ ○

4 Shade the bubble next to the **saying verb**.

○ laughed ○ walked ○ sat ○ is flying

5 Shade the bubble next to a **saying verb** that could complete this sentence.

Sergeant Wilson __________ *for volunteers.*

○ ran ○ slept ○ asked ○ thought

6 Shade the bubble below the **feeling verb** in this sentence.

Melanie loves to ride her horse Misty.

○ ○ ○ ○

7 Shade the bubble next to the sentence that is in the **past tense**.

○ I am holding the cup. ○ I will hold the cup.

○ I might hold the cup. ○ I held the cup.

8 Shade the bubble beneath the **modal verb** in this sentence.

We might go to the Royal Melbourne Show on Tuesday.

9 Shade the bubble next to the **adverb**.

- ◯ walked
- ◯ upon
- ◯ eagerly
- ◯ bright

10 Shade the bubble below the **adverb** in this sentence.

We should take an umbrella because it will probably rain.

11 Shade the bubble next to the **prepositional phrase** in this sentence.

Cass and Ravi are riding their bikes to school.

- ◯ Cass and Ravi
- ◯ are riding
- ◯ their bikes
- ◯ to school

12 Shade the **modal adverb** in this sentence.

The cat will probably catch the mouse.

- ◯ mouse
- ◯ probably
- ◯ catch
- ◯ will

How am I doing?

Tick the boxes if you understand.

- Doing verbs tell us what is being done, has been done or will be done. ☐
- Saying verbs show us the manner in which words are spoken. ☐
- Thinking and feeling verbs show what we think, believe or feel about things. ☐
- Verbs can show us tense – past, present and future. ☐
- Modal verbs and adverbs express ideas about what is possible. ☐
- Adverbs tell us more about verbs. ☐
- Prepositional phrases are groups of words beginning with a preposition and without a verb that tell us when, where and how. ☐

Topic 3: Text cohesion and language devices

Learning intentions

We are learning to use antonyms, synonyms and prefixes to make our writing more interesting and descriptive.

We are learning to use pronouns, text connectives and language devices to add creativity to our writing and communication.

Unit 3.1 Text cohesion – Antonyms

Busy Anto Nym

1 Anto Nym works for a circus. His busy day begins at dawn when he unloads the circus truck. Up goes the big tent for the show and up goes the little tent where the performers change.

2 Anto Nym's next job is to advertise the show and sell tickets. He does this by dressing as a clown and riding his "Crazy Bike" through the town. He wears a serious face but he performs funny tricks. Many people buy tickets because they think Anto is funny.

3 At dusk, Anto Nym shows people to the entrance of the big tent.

4 Anto is an acrobat. He performs on the trapeze, where he swings up and down.

5 Anto also juggles. He tosses and catches many objects at the same time. He makes juggling look easy when it is really very difficult.

6 Later, Anto helps to form a human tower with his brothers Syno and Hommy. Anto is on the top and Hommy, the strongest of the brothers, is on the bottom.

7 Late at night, when the performance has finished, Anto shows people to the exit and then he relaxes until bedtime.

8 As the week ends, down comes the little tent and down comes the big tent. Anto then loads everything onto the circus truck. He makes sure that nothing is left behind and then he drives to the next town.

Antonyms are opposites. For example: *on/off* *afternoon/morning* *peace/war*

1 Find words in the story on the opposite page that are antonyms for these words.

a loads ____________ **b** big ____________ **c** serious ____________

d up ____________ **e** entrance ____________ **f** day ____________

g begins ____________ **h** begun ____________ **i** bottom ____________

j dawn ____________ **k** tosses ____________ **l** idle ____________

m easy ____________ **n** buy ____________

2 Add the prefixes *un-*, *dis-* or *mis-* to make the following words antonyms.

a ____________ agree **b** ____________ fair

c ____________ fold **d** ____________ fire

e ____________ believe **f** ____________ hurt

g ____________ behave **h** ____________ kind

i ____________ prepared **j** ____________ known

k ____________ approve **l** ____________ real

Many antonyms can be formed by adding a prefix or changing the suffix. For example: **unhappy, invisible, misunderstood, disobey, impossible, illegal, careful/careless, useful/useless**

3 Write **antonyms** for the following words by changing the suffix.

a meaningful ____________ **b** cheerful ____________

c hopeless ____________ **d** thoughtless ____________

Try it out!

Unjumble the words in the box to make antonyms for the words below.

tcupaer	stew	gtubho	fots	yrd
eefzre	lmlas	wef	hirgt	rsuqea

a boil ____________ **b** sold ____________

c firm ____________ **d** escape ____________

e many ____________ **f** large ____________

g moist ____________ **h** left ____________

i east ____________ **j** circular ____________

Syno Nym, the acrobat

Presenting Syno Nym the trampolining acrobat ...

Syno goes up and

Syno comes down.

Syno rises and

Syno drops.

Syno ascends and

Syno descends.

Syno soars and

Syno dives.

Syno climbs and

Syno falls.

And everyone goes home with cricks in their necks.

Synonyms are words that mean the same (or nearly the same) as other words.

For example: *big – large, huge, great, massive;*
sad – unhappy, glum, gloomy, depressed

1 Use the Syno Nym story to help you write synonyms for:

a goes up ______________________

b comes down ______________________

2 Underline the word in each group that is NOT a synonym for the bold word.

a	**happy**	glad	cheerful	sad
b	**strong**	powerful	muscular	feeble
c	**costly**	expensive	pricey	cheap
d	**bad**	evil	nasty	good
e	**fast**	rapid	speedy	slow

It is a good idea to build up a word bank of synonyms as a reference to improve your writing. When you write a simple word such as **big**, think, "Are there better words that mean the same or nearly the same?"

3 Replace the bold word in each sentence below with a synonym from the box.

tidy	famous	difficult	savage	wandering
damp	free	purchased	roads	village

a Robbie's towel was still **wet** ______________________ from the sudden downpour.

b The rock star had become **well known** ______________________ in only a short time.

c Hector was asked to leave his room **neat** ______________________ before going out.

d We **bought** ______________________ our new television at the market on the corner.

e Mrs Mancini told us that the test would not be **hard** ______________________ .

f A **wild** ________________ tiger was **loose** ________________ and **roaming** ______________________ around the **streets** ________________ of our **town** ________________ .

Try it out!

On a separate piece of paper, match the words in Box A with their synonyms in Box B.

A

messy	hoax	dawn
small	odour	select
old	kind	banquet
sharp	ascend	weary
minimum	new	

B

tired	least	choose
trick	generous	pointy
smell	ancient	modern
feast	morning	untidy
climb	tiny	

Homonymbus ~~won~~ one

1

2

3

4

5

6

7

8

9
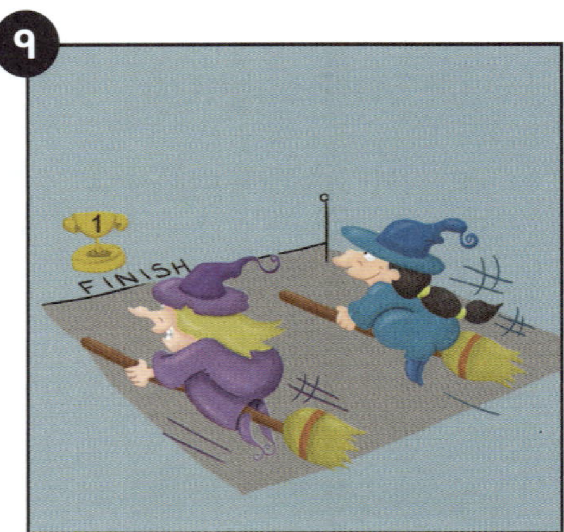

10

Homonyms are words that sound the same but have different meanings.
For example: *Sun* (the Earth's star) *son* (a male child)
stake (a stick with a point) *steak* (a thick piece of meat)

1 Write the numbers of the pictures on on the opposite page that best fit these phrases or sentences.

a A dear deer ______ **b** That's a foul fowl! ______ **c** A bare bear ______

d The nose knows ______ **e** A boy on a buoy ______ **f** A cheap cheep ______

g A leek with a leak ______ **h** What does a reed read? ______

i A thrown throne ______ **j** Which witch won one? ______

2 Circle the correct homonyms in each sentence.

a The students were not (aloud / allowed) to play (their / there) music (aloud / allowed) during (their / there) lunch (break / brake).

b Ms Sanchez (read / red) a (tale / tail) about a monkey with a magical bright (read / red) (tale / tail).

c The artist painted the (seen / scene) as she had (seen / scene) it on her recent trip to the outback.

d At the (fair / fare) we were asked to (sell / cell) tickets for people to visit the (sell / cell) in which Ned Kelly had (been / bean) imprisoned.

Homonyms can be homographs, words with the same spelling but different meanings, for example: **bear (animal)**, **bear (to carry)**, or homophones, words with the same sound but spelled differently and with different meanings, for example: **pear/pair**, **blue/blew**.

3 Write homonyms that mean the following:

a the time after the sun sets __________ ;
a medieval soldier in armour __________

b hurt __________ ; a sheet of glass for a window __________

c a small stream __________ ; a sharp squeaking sound __________

Try it out!

On a separate piece of paper, draw one of the following:

- a mussel with muscles up to his/her waist in waste
- patients losing patience while waiting to lose weight
- a three-toed toad being towed behind something with a sail that is for sale.

Tides

Have you ever battled to get a sandcastle finished at the beach before it is swamped and washed away by a rising tide? We often incorrectly say that tides "come in" and "go out" but in fact tides rise and fall. What is it that causes tides to rise and fall?

The Moon is the main culprit responsible for the movement of tides all over Earth. Being the closest body to Earth in space, the Moon exerts a strong gravitational pull on our planet. The gravitational pull of the Moon causes the oceans on Earth to bulge towards it. At the same time, Earth itself turns around the Sun and there is a gravitational pull between them. The constant forces at work in these two orbits mean that when the Moon causes water to bulge towards it on the side of Earth nearest to the Moon, it also causes an equal bulge on the other side. This means, strangely, that when there is a high tide on one side of the planet there is also a high tide on the other side.

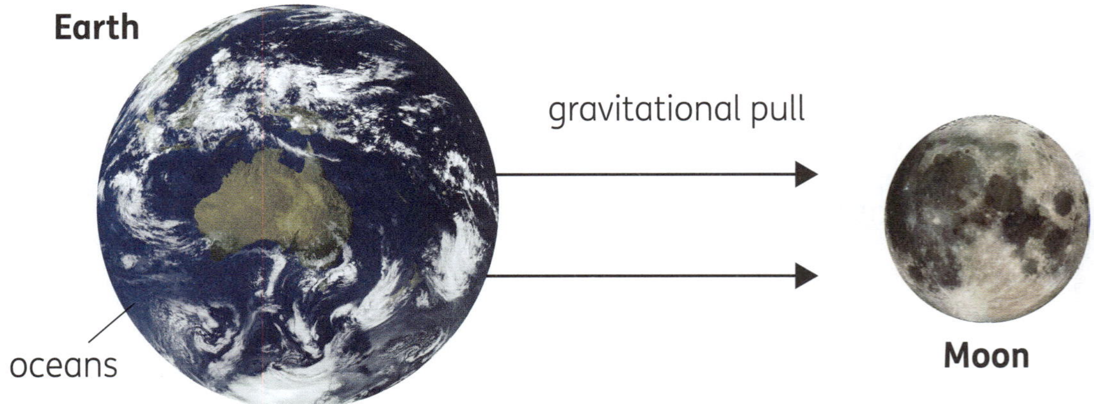

Wherever you are on the coast, there will be a high tide every 12 hours and 25 minutes, and therefore two high tides every 24 hours and 50 minutes. This is because Earth rotates a full 360° in 24 hours (that's one complete rotation per day). In the same 24 hours, the Moon rotates 12° around the Earth.

So, to be a successful sandcastle builder, it's best to begin your castle at low tide and finish it within 12 hours and 25 minutes.

We use paragraphs to organise the information we write. A paragraph is a section in a piece of writing that begins on a new line and deals with a single idea or theme. Paragraphs usually start with a topic sentence, which tells us the main point of the paragraph.

1 Number the paragraphs in the "Tides" information report from 1 to 4 and use those numbers to answer the questions that follow.

a Which paragraph tells us what causes tides? ________________

b Which paragraph introduces the information report? ________________

c Which paragraph explains how often we have high tides? ________________

d Which paragraph contains a concluding statement? ________________

2 Write the sentence from paragraph 2 that you think is the topic sentence.

____

____

____

____

____

Try it out!

The "Tides" is an information report, which is a type of informative text. Information reports tell why things happen or how something works or has formed. They organise information into bundles known as **paragraphs**.

On a separate piece of paper, write an information report about an animal of your choice.

Organise your writing into **paragraphs** that cover the following areas.

- Introduce and classify your animal: What kind of animal is it?
- Which animal family does it belong to? For instance, is it a mammal, a reptile, a bird, a domestic/tame animal?
- What does it look like?
- Where do you find it?
- What does it eat?
- Your last paragraph should be a concluding statement.

Amira's picture day

Amira peered through the window, but saw only the black, unblinking sky. "Do you see the moon?" whispered Mom.

Ziyad scanned the sky and shouted, "I think I see it!"

"I see it too!" Amira said.

Mom drew them in for a hug. "That means it's Eid tomorrow."

Amira felt warm and tingly inside. She couldn't keep still even when she tried. She rushed to bring her mom the mehndi cone.

In a few minutes, her hands were decorated with wet green swirls and designs. Her mom even doodled her favourite animal, a dolphin, in the middle of one hand with a mermaid on the other. Amira held her hands out carefully to make sure they dried. She hoped her mehndi designs would be a deep chocolate brown the next morning.

"Tomorrow, we get to skip school!" yelled Ziyad. Amira cheered.

"Okay, you two! Let's use your energy to make some goody bags," said Mom. Amira joined her little brother in counting lollipops for the children at the masjid.

Reem Faruqi

Pronouns can stand in the place of nouns to make sentences easier to read.

Some of the most common pronouns are: *he, she, it, his, himself, him, her, herself, hers, I, me, mine, yours, ours, theirs, themselves, ourselves, we, myself, you, its, itself, them, they.*

1 Read the extract from "Amira's picture day", and then rewrite the following sentences, replacing the bold nouns with pronouns.

a **Amira** peered through the window, but saw only the black, unblinking sky.

____

____

b **Ziyad** scanned the sky and shouted, "I think I see it!"

____

____

c **Mom** drew them in for a hug.

____

____

Pronouns that show us that someone owns something are called possessive pronouns.

The most common possessive pronouns are: *mine, ours, yours, his, hers, theirs.*

2 Write possessive pronouns from the box below that best fit into the gaps in the sentences.

theirs ours mine yours

a This bag belongs to you. This bag is ______________ .

b That pencil belongs to us. It is ______________ .

c The pet rabbit belongs to me. It is ______________ .

d Mr Carver judged the model show. He told the boys that he liked ______________ best of all.

Try it out!

On a separate piece of paper, write a paragraph with four sentences about yourself. Include the **pronouns** *I, me* and *mine* in your paragraph.

Ancient Greek gods

Zeus, who was the chief god, often became angry with humans. He hurled lightning bolts that would shake the Earth.

Hera, who was the wife of Zeus, sometimes tried to help humans.

She often repaired the damage that the bad temper of Zeus had caused.

Another violent god was Ares, who was the god of war. Ares loved to start battles and wars, which sometimes lasted for years.

Apollo was a handsome god who loved music and archery.

It was Apollo who drove the sun-chariot that lit up the sky and gave the world daylight.

Athena, who was the goddess of wisdom, was the daughter of Zeus. Athena was another god who tried to protect humans.

She looked after some humans by giving them special powers that helped them to conquer monsters.

Poseidon, the god of the seas, had the power to start earthquakes.
He carried a weapon called a trident that could stir up the oceans until they caused terrible and furious storms.

Hades, whose name means "the unseen one", was the god of the underworld. The underworld was a place for the dead, guarded by the three-headed dog Cerberus, who would stop the dead from returning to the land of the living.

Who, *which* and *that* can also be used as pronouns.
These pronouns can be used to tell us about a person or thing already mentioned in a sentence.
For example: *Zeus, **who** lived on Mount Olympus, threw frightening lightning bolts.*
These pronouns can also be used to join two sentences.
For example: *Another violent god was Ares. Ares was the god of war.*
→ *Another violent god was Ares, **who** was the god of war.*
Who has taken the place of *Ares* to save us repeating that name.

1 Use the pronouns **who** (or **whose**), **which** or **that** to write these pairs of sentences as one sentence. The text opposite will help you.

a Apollo was a handsome god. Apollo loved music and archery.

____

b Poseidon carried a trident. The trident could stir the oceans into terrible and furious storms. ______________________________

____

c Ares loved to start battles and wars. The battles and wars sometimes lasted for years.

____

d Hades was the god of the underworld. Hades' name means "the unseen one".

____

e Hera was Zeus's wife. Hera tried to help humans.

____

Who refers to people. *Which* or *that* are generally used to refer to places, animals, things or ideas.

2 Finish these sentences in your own words.

a My neighbour, who ______________________________.

b I saw a horse that ______________________________.

c We caught the train, which ______________________________.

d The boy who ______________________________.

Try it out!

On a separate piece of paper, change these single sentences into two sentences.

a I borrowed a library book that was all about building model aeroplanes.

b We met a lady who had just arrived in Australia from Turkey.

c Taz showed me the house that was thought to be where a wizard lived.

Yoghurt crunch

Here's a delicious breakfast recipe that can also double as an "any time" snack.

1 cup rolled oats

1 tbsp light olive oil

2 tbsps maple syrup

$\frac{1}{3}$ cup blanched almonds, chopped

$\frac{1}{3}$ cup pecans, chopped

$\frac{1}{3}$ cup chopped dried apples

$\frac{1}{3}$ chopped dried apricots

yoghurt to serve

rolled oats

olive oil

maple syrup

Method

1. First, preheat the oven to 180°C.
2. Place the rolled oats in a medium bowl and drizzle with olive oil and maple syrup, then stir to combine.
3. Next, spread the oat mixture over a baking tray and bake in the oven for 5 minutes.
4. Now sprinkle the almonds and pecans over your oat mixture, then bake for 5–7 minutes, stirring once during the cooking process. When the nuts are golden brown and crisp, transfer the oat mixture to a bowl to cool.
5. When cool, stir in the dried apples and dried apricots.
6. Finally, sprinkle the mixture over your favourite yoghurt and enjoy!
   (Serves 6)

dried fruit and nuts

yoghurt

yoghurt crunch

When words are used to sequence events, steps in a recipe or arguments, these words are called text connectives. Text connectives form links between sentences or paragraphs.

For example: ***First*** *fold the paper in half,* ***then*** *write your name on one half.* ***Next*** *fold the paper in half again.* ***Finally****, place the paper in an envelope.*

1 Read the "Yoghurt crunch" recipe and then circle the text connectives in the sentences below.

a First, preheat the oven to 180°C.

b Finally, sprinkle the mixture over your favourite yoghurt and enjoy!

c Place the rolled oats in a medium bowl and drizzle with olive oil and maple syrup, then stir to combine.

d Next, spread the oat mixture over a baking tray and bake in the oven for 5 minutes.

e Now sprinkle the almonds and pecans over your oat mixture, then bake for 5–7 minutes, stirring once during the cooking process.

2 Use time sequence text connectives of your own to complete these sentences. If you need help, you will find some text connectives in the "Try it out!" box below.

a ______________________ we put on our socks and boots.

b ______________________ we went outside to play.

c To __________________ with, I placed the ball on the ground, __________________ kicked it as hard as I could towards the goal.

d My little brother had several turns and ____________________ he kicked a goal too.

e ______________________ my cousin Jai showed us how to make a mark.

f ______________________ we are going to ride our bikes to the park.

Try it out!

Here is a list of some **text connectives**.

first, to begin with, to start with, first of all, for a start, next, now, then, soon, later, afterwards, meanwhile, finally, to conclude, in conclusion, last

On a separate piece of paper, write out a recipe or set of instructions using **text connectives** to help the reader follow the recipe in the correct order.

Fascinating food facts

Did you know that honey can never go "off"?

The acids in honey help to keep bacteria out. In fact, edible honey was found in the Ancient Egyptian pyramids. Despite the honey being thousands of years old, archaeologists found that it could still be safely eaten.

If you eat large amounts of carrots, your skin will eventually turn orange. There is no evidence to suggest that eating lots of carrots will allow you to see well in the dark; however, they will help to keep your eyes healthy.

Roman soldiers were often paid in salt. In fact, the word *salary* comes from the Latin word for "salt" – sal.

Almonds are eaten as nuts, although they are actually members of the peach family, and are therefore fruits.

You can test whether an egg is "off" by placing it in a bowl of water. As the egg ages, gas builds up inside the shell, making the egg buoyant. Because of this, the egg will float in water and this signals that it should not be eaten.

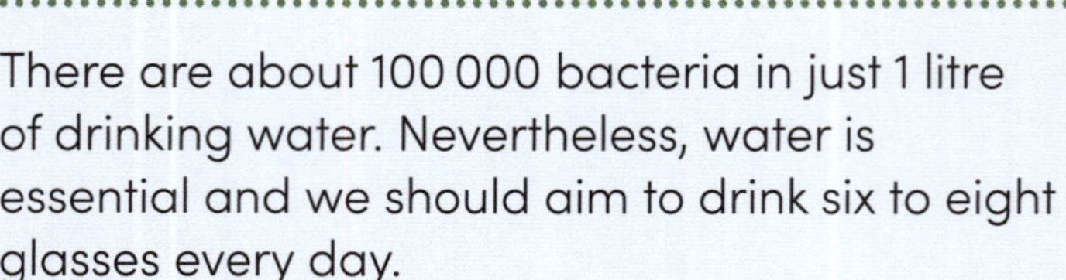

There are about 100 000 bacteria in just 1 litre of drinking water. Nevertheless, water is essential and we should aim to drink six to eight glasses every day.

The first canned food was invented in 1804 to feed Napoleon Bonaparte's army. The can opener, however, wasn't invented until 48 years later.

Text connectives are a way of showing the reader how the text is developing or what is coming up. They can link ideas together.

For example: *Hippos appear to be slow, friendly animals. However, they are among the most dangerous creatures on Earth.* (*However* is the text connective, because it links two ideas.)

1 Read "Fascinating food facts" to help you fill in the missing text connectives.

a The acids in honey help to keep bacteria out. ______________, edible honey was found in the Ancient Egyptian pyramids. ______________ the honey being thousands of years old, archaeologists found that it could still be safely eaten.

b Almonds are eaten as nuts, ______________ they are actually members of the peach family, and are therefore fruits.

c There are about 100 000 bacteria in just 1 litre of drinking water. ______________, water is essential and we should aim to drink six to eight glasses every day.

d As an egg ages, gas builds up inside the shell, making the egg buoyant. ______________, the egg will float in water and this signals that it should not be eaten.

e The first canned food was invented in 1804. The can opener, ______________, wasn't invented until 48 years later.

Text connectives can be confused with conjunctions. However, conjunctions can only be found **within** sentences, whereas text connectives form links **between** sentences or even paragraphs.

2 Text connectives can differ in their function. Circle any text connectives below that could sequence time.

first	therefore	later	however
otherwise	soon	for example	finally
nevertheless	in fact	earlier	in any case

Try it out!

Circle the words below that you think form the two **text connectives** in these sentences.

The hare is an extremely fast animal. On the other hand, the tortoise is a very slow reptile. All the same, in Aesop's famous fable, the tortoise was victorious in its race with the hare.

Strange parade

Last night I had the strangest dream
As odd as it could be.
I dreamt I was a gildfosh
Sitting in a tree.
And as I sat upon a limb
Sipping lemonade,
A weird procession passed me by –
An animal parade.
First there came two kongarees upon
their heads were crowns.
Followed by three parrokots in
chequered dressing gowns.
Then came four clomping lozrads
their feet encased in boots.
Behind them strode five pussims in
prickly prison suits.
Next prancing down the laneway six
fregs in underwear
And seven bonnie bunyoops in wigs
of long blonde hair.
Then came a feathered tiger sneak
And she did hiss to me,
"Now come on down and join the gang
From out that old gam tree."
Well how could I resist her?
That wicked, sneakish charmer.
So down I hopped and joined the troop
All in my plastic armour.

Authors often use word play to make their writing more interesting and entertaining. Some authors use nonsense words.

1 Read "Strange parade", then write sensible nouns for these nonsense words from the poem.

a gildfosh ______________________

b kongarees ______________________

c parrokots ______________________

d lozrads ______________________

e pussims ______________________

f fregs ______________________

Another type of play on words is the pun. A pun is a word play in which a word or phrase is used in a different way to make what is being written humorous.

For example: *I used to be a tailor but I found the work was just so-so.*

2 Write the endings from the box that best fit these puns.

they're two-tyred.	Go on ahead. I'll follow on foot!	free of charge.
Then it hit me!	He got twelve months!	Eventually, it came back to me.

a I wondered why the baseball bat was getting bigger. ______________________

b Flat batteries were given out ______________________

c Did you hear about the thief who stole a calendar? ______________________

d What did the shoe say to the hat? ______________________

____

e I couldn't remember how to throw a boomerang. ______________________

____

f Bicycles can't stand up on their own because ______________________

Authors also use word play such as spoonerisms. A spoonerism is a word play in which the first letters or sounds of words are mixed up.

For example: *It's a lack of pies. (It's a pack of lies.) Wave the sails! (Save the whales!)*

Try it out!

Can you identify these fairy-tale spoonerisms and write them correctly?

a The Pea Little Thrigs   b Beeping Slooty   c The Prog Frince

Unbearable!
(but funny)

Read these rather strange sports comments:

1 "He's a player not blessed with vertical height."
Cricket commentator

2 PENRITH PANTHERS POUNCE ON PADDY
Headline on sports pages

3 "The road ahead to the finals is as straight as an arrow," said the basketball coach.

4 "Let me sew you to your sheet," said the steward at the start of the game.

5 "Wham! Bang! That's another smash from Sami!" shouted the excited commentator.

6 "He's like a shark without a notion!"
Surfing commentator

When we write, we can use language devices to make our writing interesting, entertaining and even funny.

Write numbers to match the following language devices and their explanations with the strange comments on the opposite page.

A I am a pun. A pun is a humorous play on words which have similar sounds but different meanings. ___________

B I am a tautology. A tautology is when there is an unnecessary repetition of words. A tautology contains words that say the same thing. ___________

C I am alliteration. Alliteration is the repeated use of the same initial letter or sound in a group of words. ___________

D I am a spoonerism. A spoonerism is a sentence in which sounds or parts of words have been mistakenly switched in such a way as to make the sentence humorous.

____

E I am a simile. A simile is a group of words that liken one thing to another. ___________

F Onomatopoeia is the use of words that, when read, sound like the sound they are describing. ___________

Try it out!

Can you draw lines to match the **pun** joke with its **pun**chline?

A

Have you ever tried eating a clock?

What did the knife and fork say to the salad?

I couldn't remember how to throw a boomerang

I used to have a fear of the first hurdle

I knew a joke about amnesia

What does a clock do when it is hungry?

B

Lettuce begin.

but I eventually got over it.

It goes back four seconds!

It's time consuming!

but then it came back to me.

but I forgot how it goes.

Topic 3: Test your grammar

Text cohesion and language devices

1 Shade the bubble next to the **antonym** for **tame**.

- ○ time
- ○ domestic
- ○ wild
- ○ happy

2 Shade the bubble next to the **antonym** for the bold word in this sentence.

We walked towards the theatre ***entrance****.*

- ○ doorway
- ○ exit
- ○ cafe
- ○ entry

3 Shade the bubble next to the **prefix** that can be added to **behave** to make an antonym for this word.

- ○ un-
- ○ dis-
- ○ im-
- ○ mis-

4 Shade the bubble next to the **prefix** that can be added to **obey** to make it an antonym.

- ○ un-
- ○ dis-
- ○ im-
- ○ mis-

5 Shade the bubble next to the **synonym** for **weak**.

- ○ feeble
- ○ strong
- ○ powerful
- ○ fortnight

6 Shade the bubble next to a **synonym** for the bold word in this sentence.

The ***interior*** *of the building had been beautifully decorated.*

- ○ outside
- ○ hallway
- ○ inside
- ○ entrance

7 Shade the bubble next to the **pronoun** that can be used to take the place of the noun group bold in this sentence.

Antonio took his old bike out of the shed and rode ***the bike*** *to school.*

- ○ his
- ○ them
- ○ it
- ○ him

8 Shade the bubble below the **pronoun** in this sentence.

Mr Pereira tried to repair the bike but he didn't have the right tools.

○ ○ ○ ○

9 Shade the bubble next to the **pronoun** that could replace the noun group in bold in this sentence.

The boys decided to catch the bus but ***the boys*** *didn't have enough money.*

○ them ○ you ○ we ○ they

10 Write **text connectives** to correctly fit the time sequence in the following.

____________________ *crack the eggs into a bowl.*

____________________ *whisk them for a minute or two.*

____________________ *pour them into a small frying pan.*

_______________ *cook them for three minutes* _______________ *serve on toast.*

11 Shade the bubble next to the **text connective** that could be used to link the following sentences.

Nate was only a young lad. ____________________, *he had yet to turn 10 years old.*

○ Instead ○ At least ○ Otherwise ○ In fact

How am I doing? **Tick the boxes if you understand.**

Antonyms are opposites. ☐

Synonyms are words that mean the same or nearly the same. ☐

Homonyms are words that sound the same but have different meanings. ☐

Pronouns can stand in the place of nouns. ☐

Language devices can be used to make our writing more entertaining. ☐

Topic 4: Sentences and punctuation

Learning intention

We are learning to write a variety of sentences and use correct punctuation for different purposes.

Unit 4.1 Sentences

Singenpoo vs Mungo

... The competition continued for another three rounds. All with the same result. The judge called out the score. "Mungo seven. Singenpoo none."

This was terrible. We were going to lose. What was wrong? What, what, what? Singenpoo looked dizzy and upset. She was staggering around in circles.

Just then I noticed something. Mr Spock was beckoning to me. I jumped down from the stage and he whispered in my ear while Mungo was having his next turn.

I stared at Singenpoo. Then at the writing on the board.

"So that's it," I said.

I rushed over to Singenpoo and took off my glasses. Then I fixed them on Singenpoo's head by bending the arms behind her ears. "Try these," I said. "The writing is too small for you to read."

Singenpoo really looked funny wearing glasses, but she started purring. Everybody laughed.

Now maybe she would be able to read the words. Maybe we still had a chance. Just maybe.

I looked at the word on my next card. Or rather I didn't look at the word on my next card. They were just a blur. Now I couldn't read them. Nothing was going right.

I raced over to Mum. "Can I borrow your glasses?" I said. Mum handed me her glasses and I stared through them at the next word on my list.

"Elephant," I said. Singenpoo walked straight over and dabbed at ELEPHANT.

Mum and Singenpoo's fans in the audience went wild. They stamped and cheered like crazy.

"Dinghy," said Mr Cane. Mungo walked up and down, staring at the blackboard. In the end he put a paw on the word DOUGH. Everyone was quiet. Mungo had made his first mistake.

Now it was Singenpoo's turn to show what she was made of. Now that she could see properly she started to get words right. And Mungo began to make errors. The bulldog couldn't read any words with silent letters in them like COMB or KNIFE. Gradually Singenpoo started to catch up.

from *Singenpoo Strikes Again* by Paul Jennings

A sentence is a group of words that make sense on their own.

A sentence needs a subject and a verb.

A sentence must begin with a capital letter and end with a full stop, a question mark or an exclamation mark.

A sentence can be in the form of a statement. For example: *I stared at Singenpoo.*

A sentence can be in the form of a question. For example: *What was wrong?*

A sentence can be in the form of an exclamation. For example: *So that's it!*

Sentences can be made more meaningful by adding noun groups, verb groups and prepositional phrases.

1 Tick the groups of words below that are sentences.

- **a** at the writing on the board ☐
- **b** This was terrible. ☐
- **c** DOUGH ☐
- **d** We were going to lose. ☐
- **e** Mr Spock beckoning ☐
- **f** Can you see Singenpoo? ☐
- **g** Everybody laughed. ☐
- **h** said ☐

2 Complete these sentences from the story of Singenpoo.

- **a** They stamped and cheered ______
- **b** Gradually Singenpoo ______
- **c** "Can I borrow ______"
- **d** ______ ______ but she started purring.

3 Make up your own sentences using these beginnings.

- **a** On Tuesday ______
- **b** What are you ______
- **c** Help, I'm ______

4 Make up your own sentences using these endings.

- **a** ______ at the supermarket on the corner.
- **b** ______ on your holidays?
- **c** ______ for your lives!

Try it out!

On a separate piece of paper, write five **sentences** that describe an animal without using the name of the animal. Make sure you write about how the animal moves as well as its appearance. Let a classmate read your sentences and try to identify your animal.

The fisherman and the bottle

There once was a fisherman who was very poor.

One day he was casting his net for fish as he usually did.

Upon his first cast, he drew from the sea only seaweed and shells. He was very disappointed. His second cast drew only sand and mud from the sea. Again, he was disappointed. The fisherman cast his net a third time and when he drew the net from the sea he saw that once again he had caught no fish. He was about to give up when a strange object caught his eye. Trapped in a corner of the net was a bottle.

"I wonder what this could be?" he asked himself. He looked closely at the bottle. He found that it had been shut tightly up with lead. He shook the bottle but heard nothing. The fisherman took his sharp fish knife and cut the lead from the neck of the bottle. He turned it upside down and shook it, but nothing came out. He set the bottle down on the sand and as he stood staring curiously at it something strange began to happen.

Slowly a thick, blue smoke started to rise out of the neck of the bottle. The smoke spread out over the water and began to take the shape of a gigantic genie.

The fisherman trembled with fear.

"Who are you?" he stammered.

"Bow to me before you die!" roared the genie.

"But please, great master, tell me, who are you?" said the frightened fisherman.

"Bow before you die!" bellowed the genie once more.

"Why must I die?" asked the fisherman. "Have I not set you free? Should I not be rewarded rather than punished?"

"I cannot allow you to live," said the genie. "During my first one hundred years of imprisonment in that bottle I vowed that the person who released me would be made rich beyond their wildest dreams. In my second century trapped in the bottle I grew bitter and I vowed that whoever released me would feel my wrath and die. Therefore, little man, prepare to die!"

"Since I am to die," said the poor fisherman, "may I ask one final question?"

"Ask!" yelled the genie.

"Were you really in that bottle? You are huge and the bottle is tiny. I cannot believe that you could fit into it."

"That bottle was my prison for two hundred years. Of course I can fit into it!"

"Then prove it to me, oh great one," cried the fisherman.

The genie instantly changed himself into smoke and disappeared into the bottle.

The fisherman quickly jammed the lead back into the neck of the bottle.

"Let me out!" pleaded the genie.

"You will kill me if I release you," said the fisherman.

"Oh please let me out!" begged the genie. "I promise no harm will come to you. In fact, I will grant you any wish you desire." **To be continued** …

A statement tells us something. Statements begin with a capital letter and end with a full stop. For example: *There once was a fisherman who was very poor.*
A question asks something. For example: *Have I not set you free?*
An exclamation is a short sentence said with strong feeling.
Exclamations begin with a capital letter and end with an exclamation mark.

1 Finish these statements, questions or exclamations from the story.

- **a** Of course I ______________________
- **b** The fisherman trembled ______________________
- **c** Why ______________________
- **d** Let me ______________________
- **e** Were you really ______________________

2 Write complete statements to answer these questions.

- **a** Why did the fisherman tremble with fear? ______________________
- **b** How long had the genie been trapped inside the bottle? ______________________

3 Write questions to match these statements.

- **a** The fisherman used his fish knife to open the bottle. ______________________
- **b** Thick, blue smoke started to rise from the bottle. ______________________

4 In the speech bubble write an exclamation of your own that you might make to warn someone about a possible danger.

Try it out!

The story of the fisherman and the bottle is unfinished. On a separate piece of paper, finish the story in your own words. Include **statements**, and at least one **question** and one **exclamation**.

Occupations

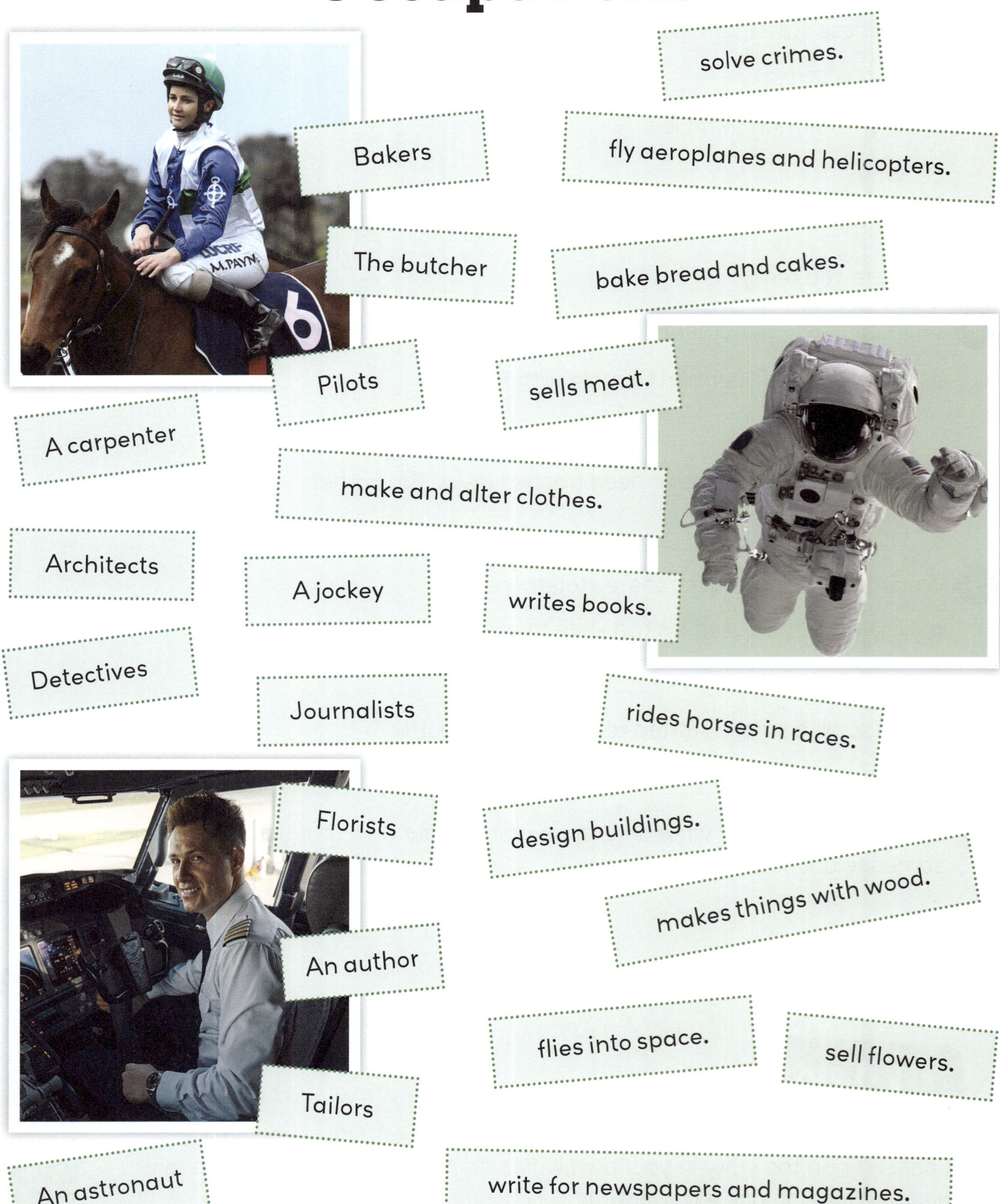

Do you remember?

The subject of a sentence tells us who or what the sentence is about.

For example: *The birds chattered in the treetops.* (Who chattered? *The birds*)

The verb tells us about the action or feelings in a sentence.

For example: *The birds chattered in the treetops.* (What did the birds do? *Chattered*)

Subjects and verbs in the same sentence must agree.

For example: *Frogs croak.* ✓ *Frog croak.* X *The frog croaks.* ✓ *The frogs croaks.* X
The children are playing. ✓ *The children is playing.* X

1 Use the labels on the opposite page to help you write sentences to match the occupations of the people with the jobs they do.

a Bakers ______________________.

b An author ______________________.

c Pilots ______________________.

d A carpenter ______________________.

e A jockey ______________________.

f Tailors ______________________.

g Architects ______________________.

h Journalists ______________________.

i Detectives ______________________.

j The butcher ______________________.

k An astronaut ______________________.

l Florists ______________________.

To agree, a **singular subject** must take a **singular verb**, and a **plural subject** must take a **plural verb**.
For example:
The dog is barking loudly.
The dogs are barking loudly.

A helping verb is also called an auxiliary verb.

2 Circle the correct helping verb to agree with the subject in each sentence.

a The cats (is/are) sleeping on the verandah.

b Theo and Mary-Lou (was/were) running to the train station.

c The red balloon (has/have) popped.

Try it out!

On a separate piece of paper, rewrite the following sentences correctly.

a Sheep was grazing in the paddock.

b The birds is flying north for the winter.

c My team are the best.

d My best friend were waiting at the bus stop.

The beach

The beach was yellow sand, but at the water's edge a rubble of shell and algae took its place. Fiddler crabs bubbled and sputtered in their holes in the sand, and in the shallows little lobsters popped in and out of their tiny homes in the rubble and sand. The sea bottom was rich with crawling and swimming and growing things. The brown algae waved in the gentle currents and the green eel grass swayed and little sea horses clung to its stems. Spotted botete, the poison fish, lay on the bottom in the eel-grass beds, and the bright-coloured swimming crabs scampered over them.

On the beach the hungry dogs and the hungry pigs of the town searched endlessly for any dead fish or sea bird that might have floated in on the rising tide.

from *The Pearl* by John Steinbeck

Conjunctions are joining words. Conjunctions can join words that are the same kind. For example, two nouns, two adjectives or two prepositions.

For example: *in **and** out* *small **but** strong*

1 Use the conjunction **and** to join words from the box to make phrases.

safe up Jill sound sweet Jack down sour

Remember that **and** is not the only conjunction (joining word). Don't make your writing boring by overusing the word **and**.

2 Use the conjunction **but** to join words from the box to make phrases.

untidy slow clean not forgotten sure gone happy tired

3 Use a conjunction to join these word pairs from the story.

a rubble ________ sand

b shell ________ algae

c bubbled ________ sputtered

d fish ________ sea bird

4 Rewrite these sentences using the coordinating conjunctions **and** or **but** to join them.

a Fiddler crabs bubbled and sputtered in their holes in the sand. In the shallows little lobsters popped in and out of their tiny holes in the rubble and sand.

Coordinating conjunctions (*and, but, so, or*) can be used to join simple sentences together to form longer, compound sentences.

b The beach was yellow sand. At the water's edge a rubble of shell and algae took its place.

Try it out!

On a separate piece of paper, complete these **compound sentences** in your own words.

a I hate basketball but ...

b ... and rode off at a gallop.

c The boat is sinking so ...

d ... but I wasn't scared.

Con Junkshun, the fruit and veggie man

My name is Con and I am a greengrocer. I sell fruit and vegetables.

I sell my fruit and vegetables in boxes and in crates.

I buy my fruit and vegetables from farmers in the country and I only buy good-quality produce.

On Sunday mornings I don't work at the market so I have time to cook breakfast for Mrs Junkshun and all my little Junkshuns.

Conjunctions are joining words.

Conjunctions can join words. For example: *fruit and vegetables*

Conjunctions can join phrases. For example: *in boxes* and *in crates*

Coordinating conjunctions can join two or more simple sentences to make one longer, compound sentence.

For example: *I wake up very early. I am always at the market before opening time, at dawn.*

→ *I wake up very early so I am always at the market before opening time, at dawn.*

1 Read about Con Junkshun on the opposite page, then use coordinating conjunctions from the box to join the sentences below.

and but so

a I sell fruit. I sell vegetables. ______

b My name is Con. I am a greengrocer. ______

______

c Being a greengrocer is hard work. I enjoy my job. ______

______

d My produce is always fresh. My customers go away satisfied. ______

______

e At 4:30 am a truck arrives from the country. I unload the produce. ______

______

f On Sunday mornings I don't work. I have time to cook breakfast for my family.

______

2 Underline the coordinating conjunction in each compound sentence.

a Lions roar but cats meow.

b I love going to the market and I am sure you will love it too.

c I might go for a walk today or I might ride my bike.

d On the way to school the car broke down so we were late.

e A greengrocer sells fruit and a butcher sells meat.

Try it out!

On a separate sheet of paper, write a few sentences telling what you would do if you had incredible superpowers. When you have finished, circle all the **conjunctions** in your writing.

Robin the Not-so-good

Somewhere deep in Sherwood Forest, Robin the Not-so-good stops a peasant who is down on his luck.

We cannot always use speech bubbles to show that someone is speaking.

When writing, we use quotation (speech) marks to show that words are being spoken.

For example: *"What time is it?" asked Riko.*

The words actually spoken by Riko are *What time is it?*

These words begin and end with quotation marks.

Use **quotation marks** to show words that are being spoken. This is called **quoted speech** or **direct speech**.

1 Fill the gaps with the words spoken by the characters in the comic strip on the opposite page.

"______________________________

____

______________________________," said Robin.

"______________________________?" asked the peasant.

"______________________________

______________________________," answered Robin.

"______________________________

______________________________!" shouted the peasant.

"______________________________!" said Robin.

2 Add quotation marks before and after the quoted (direct) speech in these sentences.

a Put that down now! shouted Mr Kumar.

b Could someone help me take down the tent please? pleaded Jiemba.

c Life wasn't meant to be easy, moaned Uncle Phil as his boat began to sink.

d Stop! commanded the sentry. No one may enter without a special pass.

3 Add quoted (direct) speech to complete these sentences.

a The phone rang so I picked it up and said, ______________________________

______________________________.

b On the last day of school we all ran through the school gate shouting, ______________________________.

Try it out!

Record a 30-second conversation with one of your classmates and then, using **quotation marks** where necessary, write your conversation down.

Matilda and the gorilla

Indirect speech

Matilda was out walking when she met an enormous gorilla. She took the gorilla to a police station and asked what she should do with the hairy beast.

Matilda was told by a police officer that she should take the gorilla to the zoo.

The next day the police officer saw Matilda walking down the street with the gorilla.

He asked why she hadn't taken the animal to the zoo as he had suggested.

Matilda told the officer that she had indeed taken the gorilla to the zoo and today she thought she would take him to the movies.

Direct speech

Matilda was out walking when she met an enormous gorilla. She took the gorilla to a police station.

"What should I do with this hairy beast?" she asked a police officer.

"Take him to the zoo," said the police officer.

The next day the police officer saw Matilda walking down the street with the gorilla.

"Why didn't you take that gorilla to the zoo?" asked the police officer.

"Oh, I did take him to the zoo," said Matilda, "and today I thought that I would take him to the movies."

Quoted (direct) speech and speech bubbles show the words that are actually spoken.

For example: *"Where are you going?" asked Tam.* The words actually spoken are *Where are you going?* The quotation marks around these words show that they are the exact words spoken.

Reported (indirect) speech is a report of what has been said. For example: *Tam asked me where I was going.*

There is no need for quotation marks because we are not writing the exact words used by Tam.

1 Fill the gaps with the exact words spoken from the story. Remember to include quotation marks where they belong.

____

________________________________ Matilda asked the police officer.

____________________________________ said the police officer.

____ he asked.

_______________________________________ said Matilda,

____

____

2 Rewrite these indirect speech sentences as quoted (direct) speech.

For example: *Bruno asked how much my bike cost.*
"How much did your bike cost?" asked Bruno.

a The old woman told me that it was six o'clock.

____

b Petra said that she was sorry that she was late for the start of the game.

____

3 Rewrite these direct speech sentences as reported (indirect) speech.

For example: *"Who's been eating my porridge?" asked Papa Bear.*
Papa Bear asked who had been eating his porridge.

a "I'll huff and I'll puff and I'll blow your house down," shouted the wolf.

____

b "Wait until the bell rings before you enter the building," said Mr Snodgrass.

____

Try it out!

Quotation marks can also be used when referring to a title. For titles, we usually add double **quotation marks** before and after the title. For example: I really enjoyed reading "Matilda and the gorilla". Add the missing **quotation marks** in the following sentences.

a Last year, I saw the movie Tobias's Pet Dragon with my friend Liam.

b Zoe chose Stargirl as her all-time favourite book.

Unit 4.8 Commas in lists

Paddy Melon's shed

Paddy Melon is tidying his shed. He has laid all sorts of things out.

a hammer

pots

a dog collar

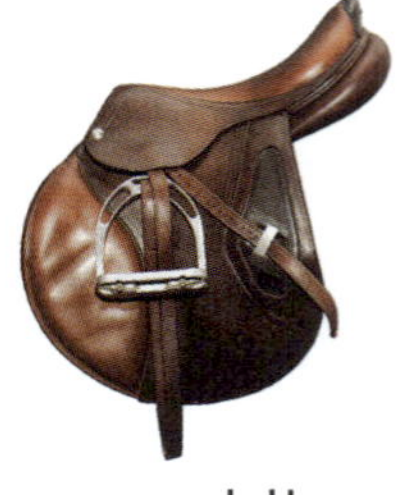
a saddle

a backpack

a billy can

a bowl

handlebars

a ladle

a saw

a tent

brakes

a cat's bowl

nails

pedals

wooden boards

a bird cage

a sleeping bag

screws

a rabbit hutch

a puncture repair kit

a dog lead

a wooden spoon

a torch

a measuring jug

A comma shows a short break or pause in a sentence. Commas are used to separate words in a list. For example: *At the grocer I bought apples, peas, oranges, tomatoes and potatoes.*

Note: There is no need to use a comma when the word *and* is before the last word in a list.

1 Use the items from Paddy Melon's shed to help you complete these sentences. Remember to use commas in your lists.

a On my camping trip I will take ______________________

______________________ and ______________________.

b ______________________

and ______________________ are all parts of my bicycle.

c To cook my soup I will need ______________________

______________________ and ______________________.

d In the box labelled "Pets" I will put ______________________

______________________ and ______________________.

e To build my cubby I will need ______________________

______________________ and ______________________.

Commas are also used to show when a reader should pause, or to separate part of the sentence from the rest of the sentence.
For example: *Mum, can I go too?*
Over on the bench, near the sewing machine, stood a strange-looking elf.

Commas can change the meaning of a sentence, so be careful how you use them. Example: **"I like cleaning, Dad," said Toni. "I like cleaning Dad," said Toni.**

2 Write commas where they belong in these sentences.

a Melbourne the capital of Victoria is a large southern city.

b My friend Barwon who is a champion swimmer is a good tennis player.

c Before we go in does everybody have their tickets ready?

d *The BFG* a book written by Roald Dahl is a really funny book.

e "Doctor can you tell me what the problem is?"

f In a cave deep in the forest lived a terrible dragon.

Try it out!

On a separate piece of paper, write five sentences containing lists of your favourite ...

a fruits and vegetables **b** people **c** mammals or birds

d TV programs or movies **e** sports, games or hobbies

Don't forget your ***commas****!*

Knock, knock

Knock, knock
Boo.
There's no need to cry, it's only a joke.

Who's there?
Boo who?

Knock, knock
Who's there?
Cowsgo.
Cowsgo who?
Cows don't go who, they go moo.

Knock, knock
Wooden shoe.
Wooden shoe like to hear another joke?

Who's there?
Wooden shoe who?

Knock, knock
Ivor.
Ivor you let me in or I'll climb through the window.

Who's there?
Ivor who?

Knock, knock
Seymour.
You'd Seymour if you opened the door.

Who's there?
Seymour who?

Knock, knock
Tank.
You're welcome!

Who's there?
Tank who?

An apostrophe of contraction is used to show that a word has been shortened. The apostrophe takes the place of any missing letters.

For example: *he's* = *he is* (the apostrophe takes the place of *i*)
we're = *we are* (the apostrophe takes the place of *a*)
it'll = *it will* (the apostrophe takes the place of *w* and *i*)

1 Write words from the "Knock, knock" jokes on the opposite page that are contractions for the following.

a I will ______________________ **b** who is ______________________

c you are ______________________ **d** there is ______________________

e do not ______________________ **f** you would ______________________

g it is ______________________

2 Draw lines to match the words in Box A with their contractions in Box B.

A

we shall
they have
I have
they will
does not
should not
I would
was not

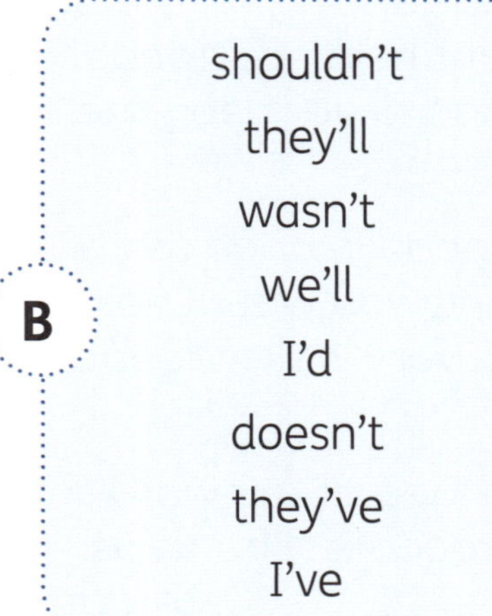

3 Copy these sentences, writing the contractions in full.

a If you don't let me in, I'll climb through the window. ______________________

____

b You'd see more if you opened the door. ______________________

____

c There's no need to cry, it's only a joke. ______________________

____

Try it out!

On a separate piece of paper, rewrite the following sentences using an **apostrophe of contraction** to shorten any words that can be shortened.

a It is your turn. **b** Do not go in there. **c** I will not stay here.

d We have done it again! **e** This is not mine. **f** They are going home now.

Crocodile and Brolga

(an Australian fable)

Crocodile was dining at his favourite waterhole. He began to cough and choke because a bone had become lodged in his throat.

"Help!" he spluttered. "Won't somebody help me please?"

Brolga, who was dancing on the plain nearby, was unsure about helping Crocodile because they had never been the best of friends.

"Help!" cried Crocodile once more. "Oh, Brolga, if only you would help me then I will reward you very well indeed. Please, oh please pull this bone from my throat."

Brolga liked the idea of a reward so she cautiously entered the waterhole and waded up to Crocodile. She thrust her head and long bill deep into the reptile's throat and pulled out the offending bone.

"Phew! That's better!" gasped Crocodile.

"Now," said Brolga, "where is the reward you have promised?"

Crocodile roared with laughter.

"You silly bird!" he said. "Your reward is that you are still alive. Few have ever lived after putting their head into my mouth."

"B ... b ... but," stammered Brolga, "I have been kind to you."

"Ah," smirked Crocodile, "a kindness is no kindness at all if it is merely done for a reward."

With that, Crocodile gave a flip of his enormous tail, turned and disappeared into the depths of the waterhole.

OXFORD UNIVERSITY PRESS

1 Write whether each of the following sentences is a statement, a question or an exclamation.

a "Won't somebody help me please?" ______

b "That's better!" ______

c "Where is the reward you have promised?" ______

d Brolga liked the idea of a reward. ______

2 Write the following as contractions.

a it is ______ b cannot ______ c will not ______

d that is ______ e I have ______ f was not ______

g you would ______ h where is ______ i you are ______

3 Rewrite the following sentences as direct speech (don't forget to use quotation marks to show the words being spoken).

a Crocodile begged for help. ______

b Brolga said that she would help Crocodile. ______

______

c Brolga asked where her reward was. ______

______

4 Underline the conjunctions in these sentences.

a She thrust her head and long bill deep into the reptile's throat and pulled out the offending bone.

b He began to cough and choke because a bone had become lodged in his throat.

c Brolga liked the idea of a reward so she cautiously entered the waterhole and waded up to Crocodile.

Try it out!

Write **commas** where they belong in the following sentences.

a Rani told us that her favourite sports were basketball soccer hockey and swimming.

b Violet indigo blue green yellow orange and red are the colours of a rainbow.

Topic 4: Test your grammar

Sentences and punctuation

1 Shade the bubble next to the **sentence**.

- ◯ in the first instance
- ◯ Harry and Katia
- ◯ He asked
- ◯ He was over there.

2 Shade the bubble next to the sentence that is a **statement**.

- ◯ Have you been invited?
- ◯ I'm invited!
- ◯ An invitation came by email.
- ◯ When will my invitation arrive?

3 Shade the bubble next to the sentence that is a **question**.

- ◯ Where are you taking that basket of fruit?
- ◯ Oops!
- ◯ I'm taking my basket to Grandma's house.
- ◯ I've dropped it!

4 Shade the bubble next to the sentence that is an **exclamation**.

- ◯ What are you waiting for?
- ◯ It's over there!
- ◯ It's so foggy I can't see where I'm going.
- ◯ I wonder if Jemma has arrived home yet.

5 Shade the bubble next to the **verb** that agrees with the bold subject in this sentence.

*The **monkeys** ________ swinging from tree to tree.*

- ◯ was
- ◯ were
- ◯ am
- ◯ is

6 Shade the bubble next to the **conjunction** that would complete this sentence.

The police were quickly on the scene ________ the thieves had already vanished.

- ◯ and
- ◯ but
- ◯ so
- ◯ or

7 Shade the bubble next to the **coordinating conjunction** that could join these sentences.

It had started raining heavily. We decided to take our raincoats.

- ◯ and
- ◯ but
- ◯ so
- ◯ or

8 Shade the bubble next to the **sentence** that is correctly punctuated.

- ◯ Did you enjoy the movie? asked Fergie.
- ◯ Did you enjoy the movie? “asked Fergie”.
- ◯ “Did you enjoy the movie? asked Fergie.”
- ◯ “Did you enjoy the movie?” asked Fergie.

9 Shade the bubble next to the **sentence** that is correctly punctuated.

- ◯ To bake the cake you need flour, eggs, butter, currants and a little water.
- ◯ To bake the cake you need flour eggs butter currants and, a little water.
- ◯ To bake the cake you need flour eggs butter currants, and a little water.
- ◯ To bake, the cake you need flour, eggs, butter, currants and a little, water.

10 Shade the bubble next to the correct **contraction** for **does not**.

- ◯ do’not
- ◯ does’nt
- ◯ doe’snt
- ◯ doesn’t

11 Shade the bubble next to the correct **contraction** for **will not**.

- ◯ willn’t
- ◯ wil’lnt
- ◯ won’t
- ◯ wo’nt

How am I doing?

Tick the boxes if you understand.

- Sentences can be statements, questions or exclamations. ☐
- The subject and verb of a sentence must agree. ☐
- Conjunctions can be used to join words, phrases or sentences. ☐
- Quotation marks show words that are actually spoken. ☐
- Commas are used to separate words in a list. ☐
- Apostrophes of contraction show that a word has been shortened. ☐

Topic 5: Using grammar

Learning intention

We are learning about the different grammatical features we find in informative, imaginative and persuasive texts.

Unit 5.1 Using grammar in informative texts

Gladiators

Rather than a game of football, soccer, tennis or the Olympic Games, the sports fans of Ancient Rome **enjoyed** nothing more than a contest between gladiators.

The word **gladiator comes** from the Latin word *gladius*, meaning "sword". Most gladiators **were** slaves, prisoners of war or criminals.

Like modern sporting contests, contests between gladiators **were held** in massive stadiums before huge crowds. One of the largest of these stadiums, the Colosseum, **can still be visited** in Rome today.

Unlike modern sporting contests, however, gladiators usually **fought** to the death. As they **filed** past the emperor into the Colosseum **to begin** their brutal contest, the gladiators **chanted** a final salute, "Hail, Emperor! We who **are about to die**, **salute** you!"

However, it **wasn't** all bad for the gladiators. Those who **survived** in the arena often **became** popular heroes, much like the sports stars of today.

Information reports, such as the one opposite, are usually organised into paragraphs, each starting with a topic sentence to introduce the main idea of the paragraph.

1. How many paragraphs are in the report titled "Gladiators"? ______
2. Read the report "Gladiators" and then underline the topic sentence in each paragraph.
3. Write **first**, **second**, **third**, **fourth** or **last** to show the paragraph that describes where gladiators fight. ______

Information reports often use simple sentences to state facts. Although this report contains a lot of simple sentences with only one verb or verb group, the author has used a lot of adjectives, phrases and noun groups to build and enrich the descriptions.

4. Look at the verbs or verb groups that are bold in the "Gladiators" report. How many simple sentences are in the report? ______
5. Complete these sentences with an expanded noun group from the report.
   - **a** ______ enjoyed gladiator contests.
   - **b** ______ is in Rome.
   - **c** Gladiators who survived often became ______ .

Synonyms are often used in information reports to describe similarities and make the information more interesting for the reader, and antonyms are sometimes used to compare differences.

6. Find and write synonyms used in the report for each word below.
   - **a** game ______
   - **b** stadium ______
   - **c** stars ______
   - **d** start ______
7. Write an antonym from the report that is the opposite of **disliked**.

   ______

Try it out!

Information reports are usually written in the present tense, unless they are about a subject that is extinct or no longer exists. Write **present** or **past** to show the correct **verb tense** for information reports about the following topics.

- **a** Snakes ______
- **b** Dinosaurs ______

What is it?

It bubbles and burbles
and gubbles and gurgles.

It's grey and gooey,
it's gummy and gluey.

It simmers and seethes
and I'm sure that it breathes!

It's squishy and slushy
and mashy and mushy.

It congeals and it clots
and it's covered in spots.

It hisses and pops
and it plips and it plops!

Oh, where should I run?
Oh, what can I do?

Dad's cooking again
and he thinks that it's stew!

Imaginative texts such as poems are often organised in verses rather than paragraphs to allow the poet to follow a rhythmic pattern of rhyming words and rhyming lines.

1 Read the poem "What is it?". How many verses are in the poem?

____

2 Write rhyming words from the poem to match the words below.

a seethes ______________ b do ______________

c slushy ______________ d clots ______________

The poet often plays with words in poems using alliteration, onomatopoeia and, occasionally, nonsense words to entertain the reader.

3 Write a line from the poem that shows alliteration.

____

4 Find and write three nonsense words from the poem.

____

5 Find two examples of onomatopoeia used in the poem.

____

Remember, alliteration is a group of words that begin with the same letter or sound. For example: **six silly sausages**
Onomatopoeia is when words sound like the thing they are describing. For example: **hisses, pops**

Adjectives (describing words) and synonyms (words with the same or similar meaning) can be used in poems to build a more interesting description for the audience.

6 Read the poem and find synonyms for the following words.

a congeals ______________ b mushy ______________

7 Make a list of eight adjectives from the poem (be careful not to confuse verbs with adjectives).

____

____

Try it out!

Write these contractions from the poem in full.

a it's ______________ b I'm ______________ c Dad's ______________

The grand reopening

You're invited!

Use adjectives to describe the exciting scene.

Pronouns such as *you*, *we*, *us* refer to and include the reader.

Use exclamations to build excitement!

Use modal verbs and adverbs to persuade the audience.

12 May, 12 pm

After three long months, the Beechwood Skatepark upgrade is finished!

You definitely won't want to miss our fun-filled family day.

You must join us for the grand reopening this Saturday afternoon!

First, Mayor Li Chan will officially open the park.

Then enjoy the FREE SAUSAGE SIZZLE and drinks and finally ...

GO CRAZY ON THOSE BOARDS AND BIKES!

Visuals such as photos show the reader how much fun the park will be.

Thinking and feeling verbs appeal to the readers' emotions.

Use text connectives to link and sequence parts of the text.

Let's investigate how grammar is used in persuasive texts such as the invitation opposite.

Use the guidelines to design an advertisement, poster or invitation of your own.

Use an exclamation to introduce your invitation and build excitement.

Use pronouns such as *you*, *we* or *us* to directly refer to and include the reader.

Use adjectives to describe the scene.

Use modal verbs and adverbs to persuade the audience.

Use thinking and feeling verbs to express opinions or appeal to the reader's emotions.

Include prepositional phrases to add details about where, when and how.

Use visuals such as illustrations to make your poster even more attractive.

Use text connectives to link and sequence the text.

Topic 6: Extension and enrichment

Learning intention

We are learning to understand and correctly use apostrophes of possession and subordinating conjunctions, as well as prefixes and suffixes, to expand our vocabulary and make our writing interesting.

Unit 6.1 Apostrophes of possession

Mixed-up matches

a

The baby's tractor

b

The bird's spaceship

c

The alien's nest

d

The pop star's cave

e

The knight's lily pad

f

The frog's castle

g

The monster's cradle

h

The farmer's guitar

We use an apostrophe of possession (ownership) to show that something belongs to someone or something.

For example: *My aunt's house* (the house of my aunt) *The dog's tail* (the tail belonging to the dog) *The school's library* (the library of the school)

1 The things belonging to the characters on the opposite page have become mixed up. Unscramble them and write the things that belong to each character using an apostrophe of possession. The first one has been done for you.

a *The baby's cradle* **b** ____________

c ____________ **d** ____________

e ____________ **f** ____________

g ____________ **h** ____________

2 Rewrite these phrases using apostrophes of possession.

For example: *the claws of the tiger = the tiger's claws*

a the beak of the eagle ____________

b the brakes of the bicycle ____________

c the pages of the book ____________

d the branches of the tree ____________

e the roar of the engine ____________

When a plural word ends in **s**, add the apostrophe of possession after the **s**. For example: **the dogs' barks** (more than one dog barking)

3 Tick the answer that shows the correct use of the apostrophe of possession.

a The boy's book was lost.

The book belongs to the boy ☐ OR the boys ☐

b The horses' hooves echoed on the cobblestones below.

The hooves belong to the horse ☐ OR the horses ☐

c The singer's notes were perfectly in tune.

The notes belong to the singer ☐ OR the singers ☐

Try it out!

On a separate piece of paper, rewrite the following sentences as newspaper headlines, showing the **apostrophes of possession** where necessary.

For example: *A truck crashed when its brakes failed. TRUCK'S BRAKES FAIL!*
Two trucks crashed when their brakes failed. TRUCKS' BRAKES FAIL!

a A girl had her bag stolen.

b Some girls had their bags stolen.

c A quick-thinking hero saves a child.

d Three quick-thinking heroes save a child.

Little Redmond and Chomper the Wolf

Once upon a time a little boy called Redmond Hood was on his way through the forest. Redmond was on his way to Granny's garage with a backpack full of motorbike parts. He was halfway through the forest when he was stopped by Chomper the Wolf.

"Where are you going and what have you got in that backpack?" asked Chomper.

"I'm off to Granny's because her Harley is sick. In my pack I have some things that Granny hopes will make Harley better," said Redmond.

Ha! I have an idea, thought Chomper. If Harley is sick, then Redmond's pack must be filled with yummy food to make him feel better. If I am very clever, I might get a free feed!

Chomper jumped onto his BMX and off he raced to Granny's place.

When Redmond arrived at Granny's garage he saw someone wearing grimy overalls leaning against the garage wall. Since he could see the name "Granny" on the pocket of the overalls, Redmond presumed it was Granny wearing the overalls.

"Oh, Granny," said Redmond, "what big eyes you have."

"I'll see an optometrist tomorrow," said Chomper (disguised cleverly as Granny).
"Now give me the pack, kid."

"Oh, Granny," said Redmond, "what big ears you have."

"My ear doctor appointment is next week," said Chomper. "Now hand over the goodies."

"Oh, Granny, what big, greasy, oily paws you have," said Redmond.

"All the better to swipe your bag," said Chomper and with that he grabbed Redmond's backpack and ran off into the forest.

These days, if you see a toothless wolf in the forest, don't dare mention Redmond and the crunchy backpack.

Some conjunctions are used to join on extra details about the main idea (main clause) in a sentence. A subordinating conjunction is used to join a main clause with a less important, subordinate clause. A subordinate clause cannot stand alone as a complete sentence.

For example: *Redmond went to Granny's house* ***because*** *her Harley was sick.*

Main clause — Subordinate clause beginning with the subordinating conjunction *because*

A clause always contains a verb. *Redmond* ***went*** *to Granny's house because her Harley* ***was*** *sick.*

Some common subordinating conjunctions are *because, when, although, since, until, while, unless, if.*

1 Read the story on the opposite page, and then complete these sentences, adding a subordinate clause beginning with the subordinating conjunction shown in bold.

a He was halfway through the forest **when** ______.

b I'm off to Granny's **because** ______.

c **If** ______, I might get a free feed.

d **When** ______ he saw someone wearing grimy overalls leaning against the garage wall.

e **Since** ______ ______, Redmond presumed it was Granny wearing the overalls.

Conjunctions can be used at the beginning or in the middle of a sentence.

2 Use subordinating conjunctions from the box to join the sentences below.

because after until

a It was a beautiful day. A cold wind started blowing. ______

______

b The trees had been chopped down. The possums had nowhere to live. ______

______

c We cannot go out. It is raining. ______

______

Try it out!

Make a chart showing all the **conjunctions** (joining words) that you are likely to use in your writing. The information box at the top of this page may help you to get started.

It's a fact!

The largest pumpkin ever grown weighed 1190 kilograms. That's roughly the equivalent of 30 Year 4 children.

The fastest of all sea fish is the swordfish, which can reach speeds of over 100 kilometres per hour.

The world's largest crab is the Japanese spider crab. Its body measures 30 centimetres across, but from claw to claw it is 3.5 metres.

The study of where words come from is called etymology.

A funambulist is a tightrope walker.

The study of mountains is called orology.

When cooking in a submarine that is underwater, the ship's cooks use peanut oil because under normal conditions it does not smoke like other oils.

Sir Joseph Banks was a botanist on Captain James Cook's journey to Australia in 1770. He gave his name to one of our country's most popular native plants – the banksia.

According to podiatrists, the average pair of feet will walk about 190 000 kilometres in a lifetime.

A prefix comes at the beginning of a word. It changes the meaning of the original word.

1 Write words from the facts on the opposite page that begin with these prefixes.

a kilo- (meaning one thousand) ____________________

b centi- (meaning one hundred) ____________________

c sub- (meaning under) ____________________

2 The suffix *-ist* means "one who can". The suffix *-ology* means "the study of". Find words in the facts on the opposite page that mean the following.

a the study of mountains ____________________

b one who studies botany ____________________

c one who specialises in the treatment of feet

____

d one who walks on a tightrope ____________________

A suffix is added to the end of a word to change the meaning of the word.

For example: *art + ist (meaning, one who can) = artist (meaning, one who can do art)*

Try it out!

Match the words in box A with their meanings in Box B

A	B
subterranean	one who studies the Earth and its structure
cyclist	a title that comes under a main title
geologist	under the ground
subtitle	one hundred years
motorist	one who rides a bicycle
subway	a supposedly one-hundred-footed insect
century	an underground passageway
centipede	one who drives a road vehicle

Tweedledee and Tweedledum

They were standing under a tree, each with an arm round the other's neck, and Alice knew which was which in a moment, because one of them had "DUM" embroidered on his collar, and the other "DEE". "I suppose they've each got 'TWEEDLE' round at the back of the collar," she said to herself.

They stood so still that she quite forgot they were alive, and she was just looking round to see if the word "TWEEDLE" was written at the back of each collar, when she was startled by a voice coming from the one marked "DUM".

"If you think we're wax-works," he said, "you ought to pay, you know. Wax-works weren't made to be looked at for nothing. Nohow!"

"Contrariwise," added the one marked "DEE", "if you think we're alive, you ought to speak."

"I'm sure I'm very sorry," was all Alice could say; for the words of the old song kept ringing through her head like the ticking of a clock, and she could hardly help saying them out loud:—

Tweedledum and Tweedledee
Agreed to have a battle;
For Tweedledum said Tweedledee
Had spoiled his nice new rattle.
Just then flew down a monstrous crow
As black as a tar-barrel;
Which frightened both the heroes so,
They quite forgot their quarrel.

from *Alice Through the Looking-Glass* by Lewis Carroll

1. Write apostrophes of possession where they belong in these phrases.

   a the others neck
   b the crows feathers
   c Alices song
   d both boys names (careful!)
   e the childrens game

2. Use the "Tweedledee and Tweedledum" story and conjunctions to help you rewrite these sentences as one longer, more interesting sentence.

   They were standing under a tree, each with an arm round the other's neck. Alice knew which was which in a moment. One of them had "DUM" embroidered on his collar and the other "DEE".

   ____

   ____

   ____

   ____

   ____

3. Change the following verbs to happening verbs by adding the suffix *-ing*.

   a say ________
   b ring ________
   c tick ________
   d come ________
   e drop ________
   f battle ________

4. Add the prefixes *anti-*, *sub-* or *bi-* to the following words to form new words and then write a definition for each.

   a ________ marine ________________
   b ________ cycle ________________
   c ________ clockwise ________________

Try it out!

Use the **subordinating conjunctions** in the box to help you complete the following sentences in your own words.

because	after	until

a Alice could tell the boys apart ________________

b They were agreeing to have a battle ________________

c We waited patiently ________________

Book 4: Test your grammar

Using grammar

1 Shade the bubble next to the **common noun**.

○ blue ○ jump ○ ship ○ quietly

2 Shade the bubble next to the correct **plural noun** for **life**.

○ lives ○ lifies ○ livies ○ lifes

3 Shade the bubble next to the **proper noun**.

○ rocket ○ Rockhampton ○ rock ○ rocking

4 Shade the bubble next to the **concrete noun**.

○ happiness ○ love ○ anger ○ battle

5 Shade the bubble next to the **abstract noun**.

○ laugh ○ laughter ○ happy ○ happiness

6 Shade the bubble below the **adjective** in this sentence.

The valiant gladiators fought bravely before the emperor.

○ ○ ○ ○

7 Shade the bubble next to the **adverb**.

○ gentle ○ gently ○ gentlemen ○ gentleman

8 Shade the bubble next to the **doing verb**.

○ wrote ○ house ○ slowly ○ Maya

9 Shade the bubble below the **saying verb** in this sentence.

"Are we there yet?" moaned the children in the back seat.

○ ○ ○ ○

10 Shade the bubble next to the word that is a **preposition** in this phrase.

over the rickety bridge

○ over ○ the ○ rickety ○ bridge

11 Shade the bubble under the word that is a **pronoun** in this sentence.

The children entered the darkened room, their torches ready.

○ ○ ○ ○

12 Shade the bubble next to the **prefix** that means **under**.

○ centi- ○ sub- ○ kilo- ○ anti-

13 Shade the bubble next to the correct **contraction** of **is not**.

○ isnt- ○ isnt' ○ is'nt ○ isn't

Complete the "Time to reflect" section on the next two pages.

Time to reflect

Tick each box when you are confident that you understand and can use the grammar listed when you write.

Understand	Use	
☐	☐	I select specific common, proper or abstract nouns to represent people, places, animals, things and ideas.
☐	☐	I choose suitable nouns to fit the topic of my writing or to represent different characters. For example: **girl**, **princess**
☐	☐	I use adjectives to describe characters and settings to make my writing more interesting.
☐	☐	I know how to expand noun groups with articles and adjectives to make my writing more meaningful to the reader.
☐	☐	I use thinking and feeling verbs to express opinions.
☐	☐	I use modal verbs such as **could**, **would**, **should** and **must** to express opinions or persuade my audience.
☐	☐	I choose suitable action, saying or relating verbs to report facts or entertain the reader.
☐	☐	I can use present, past and future tense verbs correctly.
☐	☐	I use adverbs and prepositional phrases to make interesting sentences with details about where, when, how or why something happens.
☐	☐	I use antonyms (opposites) and synonyms (similar meaning) to help describe and compare people, places, animals, things or ideas.
☐	☐	I use paragraphs to organise my writing into logical bundles.
☐	☐	I use topic sentences to introduce the main idea in each paragraph.
☐	☐	I use pronouns that agree with the noun to which they refer. For example: **Evie/she**, **the boys/they**
☐	☐	I know how to use text connectives to link paragraphs or sentences in time or sequence. For example: **first**, **then**, **later**, **finally**
☐	☐	I know how to write statements, questions and exclamations.

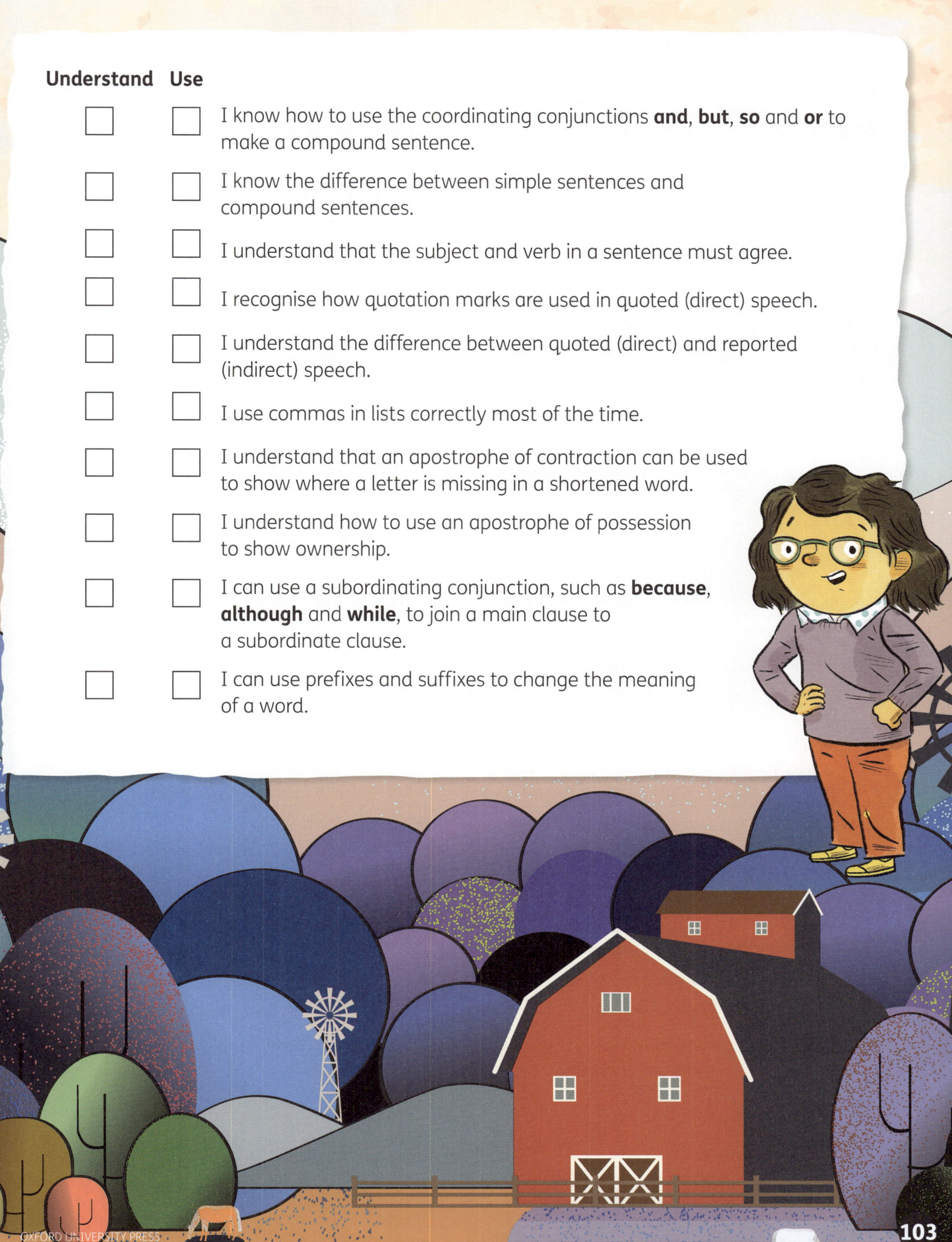

Understand	Use	
☐	☐	I know how to use the coordinating conjunctions **and**, **but**, **so** and **or** to make a compound sentence.
☐	☐	I know the difference between simple sentences and compound sentences.
☐	☐	I understand that the subject and verb in a sentence must agree.
☐	☐	I recognise how quotation marks are used in quoted (direct) speech.
☐	☐	I understand the difference between quoted (direct) and reported (indirect) speech.
☐	☐	I use commas in lists correctly most of the time.
☐	☐	I understand that an apostrophe of contraction can be used to show where a letter is missing in a shortened word.
☐	☐	I understand how to use an apostrophe of possession to show ownership.
☐	☐	I can use a subordinating conjunction, such as **because**, **although** and **while**, to join a main clause to a subordinate clause.
☐	☐	I can use prefixes and suffixes to change the meaning of a word.

Glossary

adjective	A word that describes nouns: *red, old, large, round, three*
adverb	A word that usually adds meaning to a verb to tell when, where or how something happens: *slowly, immediately, soon, here* **modal adverb** (shows degree of certainty): *definitely, probably*
alliteration	A group of words that begin with or contain the same sound: *six silly sausages*
antonym	An opposite: *full/empty, sitting/standing, front/back*
apostrophe of contraction	A punctuation mark that shows where a letter is missing in a shortened word: *isn't, we'll, I'm, shouldn't*
apostrophe of possession	A punctuation mark that shows ownership: *Bob's hat, the man's car, the boys' backpacks*
auxiliary verb	A verb that helps another verb to form tenses, questions or negatives: *She* was *playing soccer.*
clause	A group of words that contain a verb and its subject
comma	A punctuation mark used to separate items in a list, to show a short pause or to separate a main clause and a subordinate clause: *Mum, can I go? When I leave, I will take some apples, bananas, oranges and cherries.*
conjunction	A joining word. **coordinating conjunction** A joining word used to join two simple sentences or main ideas: *and, but, or, so* **subordinating conjunction** A joining word used to join a main clause and one or more subordinate clauses: *because, since, when, if*
contraction	A short form of a word or combination of words: *isn't*
exclamation	A sentence that shows a raised voice or strong feeling: *Look out! Hey you! Don't look yet!*
exclamation mark	An exclamation mark (**!**) goes at the end of an exclamation. *Hello!*
homonym	Words that sound the same but have different meanings: *see, sea* **homographs** Words with the same spelling but different meaning: *row (propel with oars), row (items in a line) and row (a quarrel)* **homophones** Words with the same sound but spelled differently and with different meanings: *pair, pear*

noun	A word that names people, places, animals, things or ideas. Nouns can be: **abstract nouns** (things that cannot be seen or touched): *happiness, idea* **common nouns** (names of ordinary things): *hat, toys, pet, mouse, clock, bird* **concrete nouns** (things that can be seen or touched): *book, pet, boy, girl* **proper nouns** (special names): *Max, Perth, Friday, March, Easter, Australia* **technical nouns** (sometimes called scientific nouns): *oxygen, carbon dioxide*
noun group	A group of words, often including an article, an adjective and a noun, that tell us more about a main noun: *the strange old house*.
onomatopoeia	Words that sound like the thing they are describing: *Bang! Crash!*
paragraph	A section of text containing a number of sentences about a particular point. Each paragraph starts on a new line.
phrase	A group of words (without a verb) that adds details about when, where, how, why: *in the car, after lunch, with a spoon, for Olivia*
plural	More than one: *chairs, dishes, boxes, cities, donkeys, loaves, foci*
prefix	A letter or word added to the start of another word to make a new word: *in- + visible*
preposition	A word that usually begins a phrase: *on, in, over, under, before, near, with*
prepositional phrase	A phrase formed when a preposition is followed by a noun or noun group: *in bed, on the weekend*
pronoun	A word that can take the place of a noun to represent people, places, animals, things or ideas: *he, she, I, it, they, we, us, me, they, them, mine* **possessive pronoun**: *mine, ours, his, hers, yours, theirs*
pun	A play on words in which a word or phrase is used in a different way to make what is being written humorous: *I used to be a tailor, but I found the work was just so-so.*
question	A sentence that asks something: *Is Tock hiding under the bed?*
question mark	A question mark (**?**) goes at the end of an question. *What is your name?*
quoted (direct) speech	The words that someone actually says. Quoted speech uses **quotation marks** at the start and end of the actual words spoken.
reported (indirect) speech	The words reporting what someone else has said.
rhyming words	Words that sound the same. *snow/flow, best/rest, dog/log*

Glossary *continued*

sentence	A group of words that makes sense, and includes a subject and at least one verb. A **simple sentence** has one main idea or main clause and one verb or verb group: *The birds **were sitting** on the fence.* A **compound sentence** uses *and, but, so* or *or* to join two main ideas or main clauses. A compound sentence has two verbs or verb groups: *Some birds **were sitting** on the fence and a cat **was lurking** below.*
simile	A group of words that liken one thing to another: *swim like a fish*
spoonerism	A word play in which the first letters or sounds of words are mixed up: *Wave the sails! (Save the whales!)*
statement	A sentence that states facts or gives opinions: *The horses ran around the paddock. I like ice cream.*
subject	The noun or noun group naming who or what a sentence is about.
suffix	A letter or a group of letters added to the end of a word to make a new word: *colour + ful*
synonym	A word that means the same or nearly the same as another word: *shouts/yells, thin/skinny*
tautology	An unnecessary repetition of a word, statement or idea: *vertical height*
text connective	A signpost word or group of words that tells how the text is developing – generally used to link two sentences or paragraphs.
topic sentence	A sentence, usually placed at the start of a paragraph, that introduces the main point being made in the paragraph.
verb	A word that tells us what is happening or being done in a sentence. Verbs can be: **doing verbs**: *walked, swam* **modal verbs** (telling how sure we are about doing something): *should, could, would, may, might, must, can, will, shall* **thinking and feeling verbs**: *know, like* **relating verbs**: *am, is, are, had* **saying verbs**: *said, asked*
verb group	A group of words that tell us more about a main verb: *might have been* wondering
verb tense	The form a verb takes to show when an action takes place – in the past, present or future: *thought/was thinking, runs/is running, will help*